New York Banker and Broker

The New York banker & broker's manual of the New York

stock, produce, mining, cotton, petroleum exchanges

New York Banker and Broker

The New York banker & broker's manual of the New York stock, produce, mining, cotton, petroleum exchanges

ISBN/EAN: 9783337120412

Printed in Europe, USA, Canada, Australia, Japan

Cover: Foto ©Suzi / pixelio.de

More available books at **www.hansebooks.com**

The

York

& Broker's

nual

of the

ining,
Cotton,
Petroleum
Exchanges.

or

0-8L

NEW YORK

The N. Y. Banker & Broker

1881.

PREFACE.

This is intended to be the initial of a periodical MANUAL, that will be issued at least annually, perhaps monthly, and which will be the most complete, reliable and convenient book of reference for all directly interested in the commercial Exchanges of New York city. Nothing will be spared to bring the information and statistics to date, absolutely correct ; any error will be owing to the neglect or refusal of the proper officials to revise proofs.

This MANUAL is published under the auspices of THE NEW YORK BANKER & BROKER, a daily record of business transactions, which assumes, as the reason of its existence, that New York is destined soon to be the commercial and financial metropolis of the world, and that this destiny will be hastened by a broader and better knowledge of the city's commercial and financial Exchanges. By concentrating all its resources on most correctly, conveniently and promptly reporting the transactions at these Exchanges, THE NEW YORK BANKER & BROKER hopes to merit its title, and win for itself and its MANUAL the cordial co-operation of all who desire New York to hold the crown of commercial supremacy.

CONTENTS.

☞ SPECIAL NOTICE.—The Digest, Security Lists and Directory are arranged alphabetically.

DIGEST

OF

RAILROADS.

ATCHISON, TOPEKA & SANTA FE.

Miles of road owned December 31, 1879		470
" " leased " "		708
" " constructed in 1880		413

Total	1,591
Capital stock, (par $100 per share)	$31,250,000
Bonded Debt	28,759,200

Semi-annual dividend of 2 per cent. paid on stock on Nov. 15th, 1880.

This company, with the St. Louis & San Francisco Company, is constructing the Atlantic & Pacific road to the Pacific.

EARNINGS.

	Miles.	Gross.	Net.
1878	868	$3,950,868	$1,883,898
1879	1,167	6,381,443	3,418,315
1880	1,591	8,543,185	

RANGE OF PRICES IN 1880.

	Highest.	Lowest.	Shares sold.
Stock	148	134⅛	810

BALTIMORE & OHIO.

Miles of main line owned		370
" branches "		56
" leased lines owned		112
" lines controlled		902

Total	1,449
Stock (par value $100 per share)	$14,792,566
Stock, preferred, (par $100)	5,000,000
Bonded debt	38,059,375

EARNINGS.

	Gross.	Net.
1878	$13,765,279	$5,995,978
1879	14,193,080	6,502,385
1880	18,317,740	7,986,970

	High- est.	Low- est.	Am'nt sold.
First Parkersburg Branch 6s....	113	108½	$37,000

Common stock paid semi-annual dividend 5 per cent. November, 15, 1880.

Preferred stock paid semi-annual dividend 3 per cent., January, 1881.

CANADA SOUTHERN.

Miles of main line owned...	230
Miles of branches owned...	170
Total...	400
Stock, (par value $100 per share)............................	$15,000,000
Bonded debt...	13,497,311

Interest on the bonded debt, at the rate of 3 per cent. per annum, is guaranteed by the New York Central Railroad Company for 20 years from 1878. The bonds carry interest at 5 per cent. after 1881.

EARNINGS.

	1878.	1879.	1880.
Gross....................	$2,480,873	$2,995,366	$3,717,277
Expenses................	2,070,258	2,448,091	2,393,051
Net......................	$410,615	$547,275	$1,324,226
Interest accrued.........	353,428	391,452	420,000
Surplus..................	$57,187	$155,823	$904,226

RANGE OF PRICES 1880.

	High- est.	Low- est.	Amount sold.
Stock......................	81¾	40	819,600 shares.
Bonds.....................	104½	88	$7,884,000

CENTRAL OF NEW JERSEY.

Miles of main line owned...	73
" branches owned...	57
" lines leased..	265
Total..	395
Stock (par value $100 per share)............................	$18,563,200
Bonded debt (7 per cent.)...................................	$53,200,000

RANGE OF PRICES 1880.

	High-est.	Low-est.	Amount sold.
Stock.......................	90¼	45	4,743,319 shares.
Bonds—First new 1890......119		113½	$237,000
First con. ass't'd....116		90	3,874,000
First conv. ass't'd...115		98	1,254,000
Adjustment..........113		105½	847,000
Income............. 97		72½	2,414,100

CENTRAL PACIFIC.

Miles of main line owned...	883
" auxiliary lines owned..................................	330
" lines leased.................................	1,147
Miles constructed and leased 1880................................	226
Total...	2,586
Capital stock ($100 par value).............................	$54,275,500

Semi-annual dividend of 3 per cent. paid on stock for 1880.

Bonded debt, funded.......................................	$57,030,000
U. S. Subsidy bonds..	27,855,680

The annual interest charge on bonds is $3,667,885.

Interest on U. S. bonds not payable until loan matures.

EARNINGS.

	Miles.	Gross.	Net.
1878..............	1,941	$17,530,858	$8,750,546
1879	2,178	17.153,163	6,945,300
1880..............	2,360	20,410,424	....

RANGE OF PRICES 1880.

	High-est.	Low-est.	Amount sold.
Stock.......................	97½	63	242,361 shares.
Bonds—1st guar............118		108½	$1,203,000
Land Grants......106½		103	142,000
San Joaquin 1st.....109		101⅜	203,000
Cal. & Oregon 1st...106½		100	163,000

CHESAPEAKE & OHIO.

Miles of main line owned.......................................	428
" branches owned..	9
Total...	437
Common stock...	$15,906,138
First preferred stock..	6,347,803
Second preferred stock.......................................	7,646,315
Total...	$29,900,256
Bonded debt bearing 6 per cent. interest....................	30,268,000

EARNINGS.

	Gross.	Net.
1878–79	$1,891,542	$384,209
1879–80	2,514,245	569,227

RANGE OF PRICES IN 1880.

	High-est.	Low-est.	Amount sold.
Common stock	25¾	15	328,053 shares.
First preferred stock	36¼	22	53,015 "
Second preferred stock	27¼	17	44,779 "
Bonds—Series B	82⅜	59½	$9,373,900
Currency 6s	51	35	9,119,500

CHICAGO & ALTON.

Miles of main line owned	244
" branches owned	122
" line leased	475
" line operated	220

Total	1,061
Common stock	$11,181,400
Preferred stock, 7 per cent. per annum, not cumulative	2,425,400

Total	$12,606,800
Bonded debt	$12,981,950

Semi-annual dividend of 3½ per cent. paid on common and preferred stock in 1880.

EARNINGS, CALENDAR YEAR.

	Gross.	Net.
1878	$4,671,519	$2,156,385
1879	5,755,677	2,706,156
1880	7,681,225	3,652,402

RANGE OF PRICES 1880.

	High-est.	Low-est.	Amount sold.
Common stock	159½	99½	105,719 shares
Preferred stock	160	117	1,077 "
Bonds 1st	125	102	$57,000
Income	117	103½	49,000
Sinking Fund 6s g.	115	108	21,000
Joliet and Chi. 1st.	108⅝	105	18,000
La. and Mo. R. 1st.	115	110	60,000
" " 2d.	101	100	20,000
St. L., J. & Chi. 1st.	115¼	112½	14,000

CHICAGO, BURLINGTON & QUINCY.

Miles main line owned January 1, 1880	675
" branches "	2,008
" line leased and controlled	97
" controlled in 1880	325

Total	3,105
Capital stock (par value $100)	$54,053,100
Republican Valley stock exchangeable January 1, 1885, (no dividends thereon until then)	$1,565,000

Dividend of 2 per cent. quarterly paid in 1880. Also extra cash dividend of $1.25 per share on May 3, 1880.

Bonded debt $54,418,725

EARNINGS.

	Gross.	Net.
1878	$14,119,665	$6,586,530
1879	14,817,105	7,588,883
1880	20,492,045	10,687,552

RANGE OF PRICES 1880.

	High-est.	Low-est.	Amount sold.
Stock	183⅛	113	350,325 shares
Bonds—1st 8s	111	108½	$377,000
7s coup	131¼	118¼	878,000
5s Sinking Fund	111	100	11,000

CHICAGO, MILWAUKEE & ST. PAUL.

Miles of road owned and leased	2,256
" constructed and leased in 1880	1,371
Total	3,627
Common stock (par $100)	$15,404,261
Preferred stock (7 per cent. per annum, not cumulative)	12,279,483
Total	$27,683,744

Semi-annual dividend of 3½ per cent. paid on both common and preferred stock in 1880.

Bonded debt $41,349,500

EARNINGS.

	Miles.	Gross.	Net.
1878	1,772	$8,451,767	$3,659,454
1879	2,256	10,012,819	4,539,025
1880	3,627	13,114,810	....

RANGE OF PRICES.

	High-est.	Low-est.	Amount sold.
Common stock	114¾	66½	5,554,943 shares.
Preferred stock	124⅛	99	169,193 "
Bonds—1st 8s S. Minn div.	111	101¼	$1,782,500
Chi. & Mil. div.	125	113	326,000
Consolidated	127	107⅞	3,124,000
Lac. & Dav. div.	102½	90	562,000
1st I. & D. div. ex.	123⅞	107½	962,000
1st H. & D. div.	120	111	973,000
1st Riv. div. guar.	128	111	316,000
1st Lacrosse div.	125	111½	383,000

RANGE OF PRICES.

	High-est.	Low-est.	Amount sold.
Common stock	130	87⅛	3,351,898 shares.
Preferred stock	146½	104	221,154 "
Bonds—Sinking Fund	112½	105⅝	$644,500
Consolidated	135½	121	585,000
1st gen	112	107¼	149,000
gen. con. coup. g	130	115	1,458,000
gen. con. reg. g	127	115¾	374,000
Winona & St. P. 1st	111	108	170,000

CHICAGO & NORTHWESTERN.

Miles of line owned	1,632
" proprietary roads	652
" road controlled	229

Total	2,513
Common stock (par $100)	$14,988,257
Preferred stock (7 per cent. per annum, not cumulative)	21,525,352

Total	$36,513,609

Quarterly dividends of 1¾ per cent. on the preferred and semi-annual dividends of 3 per cent. on the common stock were paid in 1880.

Bonded debt	$36,115,000
Annual interest charge	3,322,015

EARNINGS.

	Miles.	Gross.	Net.
1877–78	2,037	$14,751,062	$7,130,117
1878–79	2,129	14,580,921	6,873,272
1879–80	2,284	17,349,349	8,917,750

CHICAGO, ROCK ISLAND & PACIFIC.

Miles of road owned	1,052
" road leased	296

Total	1,348
Capital stock (par $100 per share)	$41,960,000

Quarterly dividend of 1¾ per cent. paid February 1, 1881.

Bonded debt	$15,000,000
Annual interest charge	950,000

EARNINGS.

	Miles.	Gross.	Net.
1877–78	1,008	$7,895,870	$3,511,356
1878–79	1,231	9,409,833	4,329,960
1879–80	1,348	11,061,662	5,265,116

RANGE OF PRICES.

	High-est.	Low-est.	Amount sold.
Stock...................	204	100½	218,270 shares.
Bonds—1st.............	100	94	$146,000
new 6s 1917 cou.	130	117	313,000
new 6s 1917 reg.	125½	113¼	239,000

CINCINNATI, INDIANAPOLIS, ST. LOUIS & CHICAGO.

Miles of road owned..	194
" " leased and controlled.................................	106
Total...	300
Capital stock..	$4,000,000
Bonded debt, interest 6 per cent. per annum.................	7,500,000

EARNINGS.

	Miles.	Gross.	Net.
1877-78...................	194	$1,309,087	$494,388
1878-79...................	194	1,342,701	507,920
1879-80...................	300	1,761,242	491,487

RANGE OF PRICES.

	High-est.	Low-est.	Amount sold.
Stock....................	89½	75	2,242 shares.
Bonds, consol. 6s.........	106	94½	$24,000

CLEVELAND, COLUMBUS, CINCINNATI & INDIANAPOLIS.

Miles of road owned..........	391
" " leased...............................	80
Total...	471
Capital stock..	$14,991,800

Dividend of 5 per cent. paid February 1, 1881. The August dividend was passed.

Bonded debt, 7 per cent. interest :

1st mortgage (C., C. & C. R. R.) $25,000 per year.............	$100,000
" (Bel. & Ind.) exchangeable for new mortgage.....	396,000
" C., C., C. & I. Sinking Fund...................	3,000,000
Consol. mortgage for $7,500,000 (Sinking Fund 1 per cent).....	2,766,000
Total...	$6,262,000

EARNINGS.

	Gross.	Net.
1878...........................	$3,528,714	$745,203
1879...........................	3,758,967	982,748
1880...........................	4,396,019	....

RANGE OF PRICES.

	Highest.	Lowest.	Amount sold.
Stock	96½	61	266,392 shares.
Bonds—1st mortgage	127	111½	$38,000
Consol	120	107	387,000
1st Sinking Fund	120½	117	70,000

COLUMBUS, CHICAGO & INDIANA CENTRAL.

Miles of main line owned... 187
" branches owned and leased..................................... 393

Total.. 580
Capital stock (par $100).. $13,938,782
Bonded debt, 7 per cent. interest.......................... 26,561,245

EARNINGS.

	Miles.	Gross.	Net.
1878	581	$3,438,665	$411,514
1879	580	3,911,261	756,300

RANGE OF PRICES.

	Highest.	Lowest.	Amount sold.
Stock	25½	9½	674,525 shares.
Bonds—1st	110	79½	$2,468,000
1st Trust Cer. inc.	107¾	78	12,282,000
Income	60	30	9,841,000

Leased to Pittsburg, Cincinnati & St. Louis, and lease guaranteed by Pennsylvania Railroad.

DELAWARE & HUDSON CANAL COMPANY.

Miles of canal owned.. 148
Miles of railroad leased... 541

The roads leased are the Albany and Susquehanna, 181 miles ; Rensselaer and Saratoga, 183 miles, and the New York and Canada, 150 miles.

Capital stock ($100 par)..................................... $20,000,000

No dividend paid since Aug. 1, 1876.

Bonded debt, interest 7 per cent........................... $19,837,000

INCOME ACCOUNT.

	Receipts.	Disbursements.	Deficit.
1878	$6,759,296	$6,818,887	$59,591
1879	7,354,475	7,985,118	630,643
1880	8,948,327	7,596,905	profit 1,35.,422

RANGE OF PRICES

Stock	Highest.	Lowest	Amount sold.
Stock	923/4	60	1,012,069 shares.
Bonds—1st reg. 1884	109¼	102½	$141,000
7s 1891	115	105	279,000
7s 1894	117½	107	287,000
1st Penn. Div	122	110¼	581,000
Alb. & Sus. 1st con.	125½	107½	490,000

DELAWARE, LACKAWANNA & WESTERN.

Miles of main line owned............ 115
" branches owned............ 93
" road leased............ 338
" road controlled............ 124

Total............ 670

Capital stock (par $50)............ $26,200,000

Quarterly dividend of 1½ per cent. paid in 1880.

Bonded debt, interest 7 per cent............ $5,677,900
Interest and rentals, 1879............ 3,624,430

EARNINGS.

	Gross.	Net.
1878	$14,454,405	$3,618,129
1879	20,226,708	3,810,451
1880	21,656,604	5,903,471

RANGE OF PRICES.

	Highest.	Lowest.	Amount sold.
Stock	110¼	68½	8,308,704 shares.
Bonds—2d	110¾	101	$56,000
Conv. 7s, 1907	125	116½	71,000

DENVER & RIO GRANDE.

Miles of main line owned Jan 1, 1880............ 251
" branches " " " 89
" road constructed in 1880............ 370

Total............ 710

Capital stock ($30,000,000 authorized)............ $16,000,000

Bonded debt, 7 per cent. interest :
1st mortgage sinking fund g............ $6,382,500
" g. Arkansas Valley div............ 1,040,000
" consol. ($15,000 per mile)............ 8,475,000

Total............ $15,897,500

EARNINGS.

	Gross.	Net.
1878	$1,124,571	....
1879	1,157,466	
1880	3,478,066	$1,710,461

RANGE OF PRICES.

	Highest.	Lowest.	Amount sold.
Stock....	88½	61¼	402,353 shares.
Bonds—1st.	116	95	$8,981,000
1st con.	116¾	90¾	6,983,000

HANNIBAL & ST. JOSEPH.

Miles of main line owned	206
"　branches "	86
Total	292
Capital stock, common.	$9,165,700
"　" preferred (7 per cent. per annum, not cum.)	5,083,024
Total	$14,251,724

The preferred stock paid a dividend of 3 per cent. in August, 1880.

Bonded debt.	$8,633,000
Annual interest charge.	654,640

EARNINGS.

	Gross.	Net.
1878	$2,045,450	$730,355
1879	1,997,465	773,943
1880	2,561,300	1,256,600

RANGE OF PRICES.

	Highest.	Lowest.	Amount sold.
Stock, common	50¾	22¾	1,341,900 shares.
" preferred	105	65½	1,043,937 "
Bonds—convt. 6s	112	100¾	$698,000

HOUSTON & TEXAS CENTRAL.

Miles of main line owned	341
"　branches "	160
"　line operated	43
Total	556
Capital stock.	$7,729,000
Bonded debt	$16,223,000
Annual interest charge.	1,177,339

EARNINGS.

	Gross.	Net.
1878-79	$3,301,681	$1,311,072
1879-80	3,499,743	1,536,565

RANGE OF PRICES.

	Highest.	Lowest.	Amount sold.
Stock	91½	49¾	254,705 shares.
Bonds—1st main line	113½	106½	$882,000
2d " "	119	105	500,000
7s Wis. div.	113	105	116,000

ILLINOIS CENTRAL.

Miles of line owned 766
"   "   controlled and leased 541

    Total 1,297
Capital stock (par $100). $29,000,000

Semi-annual dividends of 3 per cent. paid in 1880.

Bonded debt. $12,000,000
Annual interest charge   677,650

EARNINGS.

	Gross.	Net.
1878 . . . .$7,111,184		$3,015,220
1879 .7,234,464		3,195,940
1880 8,304,511		3,747,523

RANGE OF PRICES.

	Highest.	Lowest.	Amount sold.
Stock 127¾		90¼	382,134 shares.

INDIANA, BLOOMINGTON & WESTERN.

Miles of road owned.   202
"   "   rented   10

    Total 212
Capital stock, common. $2,500,000
"   "   scrip.   30,000
Bonded debt. $7,500,000
Annual interest charge   382,000

EARNINGS.

	Miles.	Gross.	Net.
1877-78	834	$1,342,523	$308,079
1878-79 . .	202	1,065,688	373,700
1879-80 .	202	1,186,347	491,008

RANGE OF PRICES.

	Highest.	Lowest.	Amount sold.
Stock	52	25	70,823 shares.
Bonds—1st g.	90	69	$500,500
1st pref . . .	123	113	30,000
2d g.	70¼	58	495,100
income.	72	42	2,540,500

INTERNATIONAL & GREAT NORTHERN.

Miles of lines owned January 1, 1881 621
Bonded debt :
First mortgage bonds 6 per cent · $6,434,000
Income bonds   5,534,000

    Total $11,968,000
Annual interest charge   835,040
First mortgage :
Income 8 per cent. if earned from earnings of 1880, 5 per
cent. declared $276,700

EARNINGS.

	Miles.	Gross.	Net.
1878	519	$1,636,585	$571,983
1879	519	1,775,861	578,087
1880	609	1,973,582	709,200

RANGE OF PRICES.

	Highest.	Lowest.	Amount sold.
Stock	50½	37½	6,098 shares.
Bonds—1st	107	99½	$623,000
Income	91	69	960,000

LAKE ERIE & WESTERN.

Miles of road owned	386
Capital stock	$7,700,000
Bonded debt	7,727,000
Annual interest charge (absolute)	258,900

GROSS EARNINGS.

1879	$695,259
1880	1,303,725

RANGE OF PRICES 1880.

	Highest.	Lowest.	Amount sold.
Stock	42¾	20¼	781,946 shares.
Bonds—1st	107¾	93½	$1,331,000
inc. 7s	73	54	3,375,000
Laf., Bl. & M. 1st.	106	61	1,391,000
" " Inc.	74¾	67	443,000

The company is a consolidation of the Lafayette, Bloomington & Muncie and the Lake Erie & Western, effected December 12, 1879.

LAKE SHORE & MICHIGAN SOUTHERN.

Miles of main line owned	540
" branches owned	484
" line leased	153
Total	1,177
Capital stock	$43,466,500
Guaranteed 10 per cent. stock	533,500
Total	$50,000,000

Semi-annual dividends of 4 per cent. on the common and of 5 per cent. on the guaranteed stock were paid in 1880. On and after May 1, 1881, dividends on common stock will be paid quarterly.

Bonded debt	$37,930,000
Annual interest charge	2,598,455

EARNINGS.

	Gross.	Net.
1878	$13,979,766	$5,493,165
1879	15,271,492	6,336,968
1880	18,720,000	8,310,000

RANGE OF PRICES 1880.

	High-est.	Low-est.	Amount sold.
Common stock	139⅝	95	5,428,252 shares.
Bonds—nc. 1st	133	118¾	$561,000
" 2d	125	114¼	371,000
Buf. & E. ext. new.	123	108	156,000
Cl. & Tol. S. F.	112	108	125,000
" 2d new.	118	107	8,000

LOUISVILLE & NASHVILLE.

Miles of main line owned	435
" branches owned	477
" road leased	554
" " controlled	912

Total operated	2,378

Capital stock (par §100)............................§18,118,800

A stock dividend of 100 per cent. was paid Dec. 1, 1880.

Bonded debt	$43,862,970
Annual interest charge	2,050,900

EARNINGS.

	Gross.	Net.
1877–78	$5,607,599	$2,344,243
1878–79	5,387,596	2,231,772
1879–80	7,435,843	3,227,643

RANGE OF PRICES 1880.

	High. est.	Low-est.	Amount sold.
Stock	174	*77	346,202 shares.
Bonds—consol	121	113	$248,000
2d gold	106½	103	181,000
Cecilian branch	110	106	10,000
general 6s	106¼	102⅝	587,000
N. O. & M. div	104	100½	134,000
Nash. & Decatur	115	106½	79,000

* Ex-dividend of 100 per cent. in stock.

MANHATTAN ELEVATED.

Miles of road operated	44
Capital Stock	§13,000,000

The company leases and operates the lines of the New York and the Metropolitan companies. It guarantees 6 per cent. per annum on $21,000,000 of bonds and 10 per cent. on $13,-000,000 of stock of these companies.

EARNINGS OF LEASED LINES.
(Year ended September 30, 1880.)

	Gross.	Net.
New York	$2,592,665	$1,165,465
Metropolitan	2,021,294	814,794
Total	$4,613,959	$1,980,259

After payment of interest on the bonds there would be left applicable to dividends on stock as follows :

New York	$636,165	9 79-100 per cent.
Metropolitan	205,344	3 16-100 per cent.

RANGE OF PRICES 1880.

	Highest.	Lowest.	Amount sold.
Stock	57½	21	1,677,534 shares.

METROPOLITAN ELEVATED.

Miles of road owned (double track)................................18¼
Capital stock (par $100).......................................$6,500,000

Quarterly dividend of 2½ per cent. paid January 1, 1881.

Bonded debt (interest 6 per cent.) :
1st mortgage...$8,500,000
2d   "   (guaranteed by Manhattan)...................... 4,000,000

Total...$12,500,000

The road is leased to the Manhattan company at a rental of 10 per cent per annum on the stock and interest on the bonds.

RANGE OF PRICES 1880.

	Highest.	Lowest.	Amount sold.
Stock	121	83	145,742 shares.
Bonds—1st	106½	100¼	$9,827,000
2d	95	91½	113,000

MICHIGAN CENTRAL.

Miles of line owned.. 270
"   leased.. 534

Total... 804
Capital stock (par $100).....................................$18,738,204

Paid semi-annual dividends of 4 per cent. in 1880.

Bonded debt...$21,113,700
Annual interest and rent charge.............................. 1,602,910

EARNINGS.

	Gross.	Net.
1878	$6,872,094	$2,504,850
1879	7,345,700	2,715,836
1880	9,100,000	3,370,000

RANGE OF PRICES 1880.

	High-est.	Low-est.	Amount sold.
Stock	130¼	75	1,412,160 shares.
Bonds—cons. 7s	129½	116¾	$493,000
1st S. F. 8s	115	106	212,000

MISSOURI, KANSAS & TEXAS.

Miles of main line owned... 576
  "   branches owned.. 232

Total.. 808

Capital stock (par $100)...................................$21,405,000

On November 17, 1880, the stockholders voted to increase the stock $25,000,000 to make extensions to Rio Grande River, City of Mexico, and Fort Smith, Ark.

Bonded debt...$26,744,553
Annual interest charge.. 1,455,000

A new consolidated mortgage for $45,000,000 has been authorized.

EARNINGS.

	Gross.	Net.
1878	$2,981,681	$428,833
1879	3,344,291	1,140,439
1880	4,163,070	....

RANGE OF PRICES 1880.

	High-est.	Low-est.	Amount sold.
Stock	49¼	28½	3,764,881 shares.
Bonds—cons. ass't	114½	92½	$20,458,000
2d income	79¾	47½	59,092,000
H. & Cen. Mo. 1st	111	108¼	33,000

MOBILE & OHIO.

Miles of main line owned... 472
  "   branches owned.. 34

Total.. 506

Capital stock (par $100)...................................$5,320,600
Bonded debt...16,250,000

Interest on $7,000,000 at 6 per cent. gold, remainder at 7 per cent.

EARNINGS.

	Miles.	Gross.	*Net.
1877–78	529	$2,098,540	$376,821
1878–79	506	1,830,620	379,468
1879–80	506	2,284,615	824,966

*After deducting all expenses, including extraordinary.

RANGE OF PRICES 1880.

	Highest.	Lowest.	Amount sold.
Stock	29¼	12	183,933 shares.
Bonds—1st new	110	95¾	$920,000
1st deb	90	68	6,257,600
2d deb	58	36	2,034,500
3d deb	45	27	494,500
4th deb	44	30	432,000

MORRIS & ESSEX.

Miles of main line owned	84
" branches owned	34
Total	118
Capital stock ($50 par)	$15,000,000

Semi-annual dividends of 3½ per cent. paid in 1880.

Bonded debt	$19,923,000
Annual interest charge, 7 per cent	1,394,610

EARNINGS.

	Gross.	Net.
1878	$2,710,117	$782,828
1879	3,515,097	1,559,354

The road is leased in perpetuity to the Delaware, Lackawanna & Western Railroad, the lessee assuming all liabilities and paying 7 per cent. per annum on the stock, and if the Morris & Essex earns 10 per cent. in any one year after 1874, it is to pay 8 per cent.

RANGE OF PRICES 1880.

	Highest.	Lowest.	Amount sold.
Stock	123	100	225,550 shares.
Bonds—1st	135	125	$116,000
2d	117¾	112	89,000
construction	121½	99½	26,000
7s of 1871	117¼	111½	102,000

NASHVILLE, CHATTANOOGA & ST. LOUIS.

Miles of main line owned..321
" branches owned.. 27
" proprietary lines..105

Total..453
Capital stock (par $25)..$6,848,899

A semi-annual dividend of 2 per cent. paid in 1880.

Bonded debt...$7,510,000
Annual interest charge.. 479,200

EARNINGS.

	Gross.	Net.
1877-78	$1,871,809	$767,995
1878-79	1,736,723	715,135
1879-80	2,099,155	914,407

RANGE OF PRICES 1880.

	Highest.	Lowest.	Amount sold.
Stock	128	47½	1,615,004 shares.
Bonds—1st	121	105	$339,000

NEW YORK CENTRAL & HUDSON RIVER.

Miles of line owned...740
" leased...260

Total...1,000
Capital stock (par $100)..$89,428,300

Quarterly dividends of 2 per cent. paid in 1880.

Bonded debt...$39,733,933
Annual interest charge.. 3,335,813

EARNINGS.

(Year ended September 30.)

	Gross.	Net.	Surplus.
1878	$28,910,555	$8,038,445	$898,917
1879	23,396,583	7,594,485	454,957
1880	33,175,913	10,569,219	3,427,706

RANGE OF PRICES 1880.

	Highest.	Lowest.	Amount sold.
Stock	155¾	122	1,756,393 shares.
Bonds—6s 1883	107	103	$328,000
6s 1887	112½	107	48,000
1st 7s coup	137	123¾	648,000
" reg	133	123½	505,000
H. R. 2d S. F. 7s	113	109½	51,000
Harlem 1st coup.	133	123½	120,000
" reg	133	124	186,000

NEW YORK CITY ELEVATED.

Miles o line owned.. 17½
Capital stock, ($100 par).................................$6,500,000

Quarterly dividend of 2½ per cent. paid April 1, 1881.

Bonded debt (interest 7 per cent)..........................$8,500,000

The road is leased to the Manhattan Company at an annual rental of 10 per cent. on the stock and interest on the bonds.

RANGE OF PRICES 1880.

	High-est.	Low-est.	Amount sold.
Stock...................	127¼	109	56,380 shares.
Bonds—1st...............	120	110	$2,201,000

NEW YORK & HARLEM.

Miles of line owned..127
"   horse car line owned.............................5½

Total...132½

Common stock ($50 par)..........................$7,950,000
Preferred   "   (")..........................1,500,000

Total...$9,450,000

Paid semi-annual dividends of 4 per cent. in 1880.

Bonded debt, 7 per cent..........................$11,109,625

The road, excepting the horse car line, is leased to the New York Central & Hudson River Railroad at an annual rental of 8 per cent. on the stock and the interest on the bonded debt The earnings are included in those of the latter road. An extra dividend is paid out of the earnings of the horse car railroad in April of each year.

RANGE OF PRICES 1880.

	High-est.	Low-est.	Amount sold.
Stock......................	196	158	8,081 shares.
Bonds—1st coupon........	133	123½	$120,000
1st regis..........	133	124	186,000

NEW YORK, LAKE ERIE & WESTERN.

```
Miles of main line owned.............................................  430
  "     branches owned...........................................  101
  "     road leased...............................................  442
  "       "   controlled............................................   86

  Total..........................................................1,009
Common stock (par $100)...............................$77,083,800
Preferred   "   (par $100)..............................  8,156,725

  Total.............................................$85,240,525
Bonded debt.........................................$70,173,744
Annual interest charge 1880–81..........................$4,149,091
   "       "       "    1881–82...........................  4,149,091
   "       "       "    1882–83...........................  4,177,749
   "       "       "    1883–84...........................  4,235,065
```

EARNINGS.

(Year ended September 30.)

	Gross.	Net.
1878	$15,644,978	$5,009,114
1879	15,942,022	4,767,323
1880	18,693,109	7,049,184

RANGE OF PRICES 1880.

	Highest.	Lowest.	Amount sold.
Common stock	51⅝	30	14,307,057 shares.
Preferred "	93½	47	603,274 "
Bonds—Erie 1st exten.	128	119¾	$116,300
" 2d "	109½	103½	105,000
" 3d "	109½	105	153,000
" 4th "	107¾	101	281,000
" 5th "	112¾	109	87,500
" 1st con. gold.	130½	115½	10,546,000
N. Y., L. E. & W. new 2d consol.	102⅞	77⅛	172,451,500
N. Y., L. E. & W. 2d con. fund.	98	71	16,171,500

NEW YORK & NEW ENGLAND.

```
Miles of main line owned.................................................208
  "     branches   "   ...............................................  57
        road leased......................................................120

  Total...............................................................385
Capital stock ($20,000,000 authorized).........................$7,146,000
Bonded debt (mortgage $10,000,000).............................$6,968,000
```

The company is the successor of the Boston, Hartford & Erie.

EARNINGS.

	Gross.	Net.
1877-78	$1,006,287	$197,890
1878-79	1,971,536	486,329
1879-80	2,324,940	628,856

RANGE OF PRICES 1880.

	High-est.	Low-est.	Amount sold.
Bonds—B., H. & E. 1st	60	35	$16,593,000
" " guaran	43¼	40	79,000

NEW YORK, NEW HAVEN & HARTFORD.

Miles of main line owned..128
    "   branches   " 18
    "   road leased.. 62

Total..203
Capital stock (par $100)....................................$15,500,000

Paid semi-annual dividends of 5 per cent. in 1880.

Bonded debt:—Harlem & Portchester 1st mort. guar...........$2,000,000

The company has no debt of its own, but guarantees the bonds of the Harlem & Portchester, which it leases.

EARNINGS.

	Gross.	Net.
1877-78	$3,817,281	$1,648,788
1878-79	3,912,743	1,670,862
1879-80	4,252,814	1,653,565

RANGE OF PRICES 1880.

	High-est.	Low-est.	Amount sold.
Stock	180	155	6,308 shares

NEW YORK, ONTARIO & WESTERN.

Miles of main line owned...249
    "   branches   " 95

Total..344
Preferred stock.. $2,000,000
Common   " 58,120,000

Total..$60,120,000

The company was organized January 22, 1880, and took the New York & Oswego Midland Railroad, which was sold under foreclosure. The bondholders and creditors of the New York & Oswego Midland took stock in the new company for their claims.

EARNINGS.

	Gross.	Net.
1877–78	$560,020	$53,662
1878–79	523,592	35,713

RANGE OF PRICES 1880.

	High-est.	Low-est.	Amount sold.
Common stock	32⅝	20	1,969,564 shares.
Preferred "	85⅜	72⅛	1,864 "

NORTHERN PACIFIC.

```
Miles of main line owned.............................................532
  "    branches    "  ..............................................31
  "    main line leased.............................................135
Own ½ interest in...................................................24

  Total on which earnings are reported..............................722
Miles constructed on April 1, 1881, on Missouri & Pend d'Oreille Di-
visions and Casselton Branch (no earnings yet reported...........266

  Total miles built.................................................988

Capital stock (par $100)..........................................
Preferred  "  (8 per cent., not cumulative)...................$42,677,537
Common    "  ................................................ 49,000,000
                                                              -----------
                                                              $91,677,537

Bonded debt, 6 per cent. interest Dec. 31, 1880.......... .....$3,881,833
```

A new consolidated mortgage for $40,000,000, 6 per cent. interest, was executed Jan. 1, 1880. A syndicate subscribed for $10,000,000, with the privilege of taking $10,000,000 more yearly for the following three years, to complete the road, and has taken $20,000,000.

EARNINGS.

	Gross.	Net.
1878–79 (10 months)	$1,167,261	$455,798
1879–80	2,230,181	709,088

RANGE OF PRICES 1880.

	High-est.	Low-est.	Amount sold.
Common stock	36	20	435,152 shares.
Preferred "	67½	39⅜	759,090 "

OHIO CENTRAL.

Miles of road owned and completed................................200
When completed will be..226
Capital stock (par $100)......................................$12,000,000

Was increased from $4,400,000 in December, 1880, to purchase $5,000,000 Ohio Central Coal Company's stock.

Bonded Debt (First Mortgage 6s)...........................$6,900,000
Annual interest charge....................................... 414,000

RANGE OF PRICES 1880.

	Highest.	Lowest.	Amount sold.
Stock....................	28⅛	13	124,244 shares.
Bonds—1st.............	107	89	$2,391,000
Income..........	60¾	44	3,395,000
Terminal Trust..102¾		99½	131,000

OHIO & MISSISSIPPI.

Miles of main line owned.............. 393
" Springfield Division......................................222

Total................ 615

Common stock (par $100)....................................$20,000,000
Preferred " (par $100) 7 per cent., cumulative........... 4,030,000

$24,030,000

The last dividend paid on the preferred stock was on March 1, 1875.

Bonded debt...$12,750,850
Annual interest charge....................................... 898,440

EARNINGS.

	Gross.	Net.
1878............	$3,136,836	$864,548
1879............	3,502,239	1,051,418
1880............		1,256,709

RANGE OF PRICES 1880.

	Highest.	Lowest.	Amount sold.
Common stock...........	44½	23	2,973,569 shares.
Preferred "	102	57½	137,655 "
Bonds—1st Consol.......	122	111	$78,000
Sink. Fund......	119	110	263,000
2d Sink. Fund...	122¼	107½	930,000
1st Spring. Div..	119¼	83	556,000
2d Mortgage....	122½	116	118,000

PANAMA.

Miles of road owned.................... 48
Capital stock (par $100) $7,000,000

Paid a quarterly dividend of 4 per cent. in November, 1880.

Bonded debt...$6,969,000
Annual interest charge........... 457,830

EARNINGS.

	Net.	Total Income.	Surplus.
1878	$1,227,292	$1,582,448	$239,627
1879	1,202,144	1,651,749	210,957

RANGE OF PRICES 1880.

	Highest.	Lowest.	Amount sold.
Stock	225	168	7,690 shares.

PHILADELPHIA & READING.

Miles of main line owned.. 98
    "   branches   " 233
    "   road leased..495
    "   "   controlled...66

Total....· 892
Common stock (par $50)......................................$32,726,375
Preferred   "   (par $50)...................................... 1,551,800

Total...$34,278,175
Bonded debt (railroad)....................................... $83,097,433
Receivers' certificates... 1,800,000
Coal & Iron Company.... 14,767,500

Total.. .... $99,664,933

EARNINGS.

	Gross.	Net.
1877–78	$11,539,593	$4,419,591
1878–79	13,106,352	4,161,763

RANGE OF PRICES.

	Highest.	Lowest.	Amount sold.
Stock	72⅜	13½	2,402,650 shares.

On May 24, 1880, Franklin B. Gowen, Edwin M. Lewis and Stephen A. Caldwell were appointed Receivers of the railroad and coal companies. On July 1, 1880, a bill was filed to foreclose the general mortgage of 1874 for $19,686,000, covering 750 miles of road.

PITTSBURG, FORT WAYNE & CHICAGO.

Miles of road owned.. 468
Capital stock .
  Guaranteed..$19,714,285
  Special improvement, guar................................... 6,461,500
           Total...$26,175,785
Bonded debt...$13,510,000
Annual interest charge...................................... 955,700

The road is leased to the Pennsylvania Company at a rental equivalent to interest on the bonded debt, sinking fund and 7 per cent. on the guaranteed stock, amounting to $19,714,285.

Quarterly dividends of 1¾ per cent. have been paid on both classes of stock since the lease in 1869.

EARNINGS.

	Gross.	Net.
1878	$7,872,476	$3,529,085
1879	8,461,563	3,729,298

RANGE OF PRICES 1880.

	Highest	Lowest	Amount sold.
Stock	125	112	5,481 shares.
Bonds—1st	140	125	$104,500
2d	130½	120¾	130,000
3d	121	118	68,000
4th	112½	112½	17,000

ROME, WATERTOWN & OGDENSBURG.

Miles of main line owned.................................... 141
  "   branches owned................................... 239
  "   line leased....................................... 29
           Total... 409
Capital stock...$5,293,900

No dividend paid since 1875.

Bonded debt..$8,066,000

Interest at 7 per cent. per annum.

Default in interest on consolidated bonds ($5,122,000) since April 1, 1878.

EARNINGS.

	Gross.	Net.
1877–78	$1,203,786	$350,747
1878–79	1,143,288	308,648
1879–80	1,467,894	487,738

RANGE OF PRICES 1880.

	High-est.	Low-est.	Amount sold.
Stock	35	19⅞	15,291 shares.
Bonds—1st consol.	81½	54	$7,850,000

ST. LOUIS, ALTON & TERRE HAUTE.

Miles of main line owned	189
" branches owned	19
" lines leased	106
Total	**314**

Capital stock:

Common	$2,300,000
Preferred, (7 per cent. cumulative)	2,468,000
Total	**$4,768,000**

A dividend of 3 per cent. was declared in January, 1881, on the preferred stock.

Bonded debt	$6,700,000
Annual interest charge	469,000

The main line is leased to the Indianapolis & St. Louis Railroad at a rental of 30 per cent. of the gross earnings up to $2,000,000, 25 per cent. on the next $1,000,000 and 20 per cent. on all over $3,000,000, but in no year is the rental to be less than $450,000.

GROSS EARNINGS.

	1879.	1880.
Main line	$1,040,023	$1,417,663
Branches	565,602	729,078

RANGE OF PRICES 1880.

	High-est.	Low-est.	Amount sold.
Stock, common	42	15	70,639 shares.
" pref.	112	42½	38,587 "
Bonds—1st	115	111¼	$35,500
2d pref.	109	100½	106,000
2d income	100	89¼	306,500

ST. LOUIS, IRON MOUNTAIN & SOUTHERN.

Miles of main line owned	490
" branches owned	195
Total	**685**
Capital stock	$21,291,296
Bonded debt	$30,041,657
Annual interest charge	2,047,799

EARNINGS.

	Gross.	Net.
1878.	$4,514,321	$1,945,956
1879.	5,292,611	2,300,655
1880.	6,265,097	2,189,871

RANGE OF PRICES 1880.

	Highest.	Lowest.	Amount sold.
Stock	66	34½	2,084,270 shares.
Bonds—1st coup	119	113	$386,000
2d gold	110	97	3,961,000
1st pref. inc.	92½	75	4,693,500
2d pref. inc.	99¼	67½	11,324,000
Ark. br. 1st guar.	112¾	99½	355,000
C. Ark. & J. 1st g.	109	97½	631,000
C. & F. 1st guar.	114½	98	1,324,000

ST. LOUIS & SAN FRANCISCO.

Miles of main line owned	370
" branches owned	227
Total	597

Capital stock:
First preferred	$4,500,000
Preferred	10,000,000
Common	10,500,000
	$25,000,000
Bonded debt	$17,900,000
Annual interest charge	863,964

Under an agreement with the Atchison, Topeka & Santa Fe a line is being constructed from Albuquerque to San Francisco, to cost $25,000,000, and to be known as the Atlantic & Pacific Railway. The issue of bonds for this purpose is to be divided between the two companies, and also the profits from operating the extension.

EARNINGS.

	Gross.	Net.
1878.	$1,201,651	$626,143
1879.	1,672,437	948,494
1880.	2,698,370	1,534,922

RANGE OF PRICES 1880.

	Highest.	Lowest.	Amount sold.
Stock—Common	48	25¼	151,051 shares.
Preferred	65	33	218,974 "
First Preferred	100	60	78,709 "
Bonds—1st Pac. Missouri	106½	97¾	$261,500
2d Class, A	100½	87¼	556,600
" B	89⅞	68	932,500
" C	87	65	1,087,000
Equipment	104¼	100	292,000

TEXAS & PACIFIC.

Miles of road owned.. 444
Capital stock ($50,000,000 authorized)......................$7,902,500
Bonded debt..$25,829,570
Annual interest charge...................................... 1,320,470

EARNINGS.

	Gross.	Net.
1877-78	$2,331,310	$708,138
1878-79	2,136,143	544,916
1879-80	2,589,220	1,045,703

RANGE OF PRICES 1880.

	High-est.	Low-est.	Amount sold.
Stock	47⅜	40	6,334 shares.
Bonds—Rio Grande Division	100	80½	$5,318,000
1st	108	106	17,000
Consol	103	90½	200,000
Income and L. Grant	88½	56	12,206,000
Construction	85	80	249,000

UNION PACIFIC.

Miles of road owned (U. P.).....................................1,042
"   "   "   (K. P.)... 677
"   "   "   (D. P)... 106

Total...1,825
Capital stock................................:..................$50,762,300

A quarterly dividend of 1½ per cent. was paid on January 1, 1881.

Bonded debt.. $82,623,114
United States Subsidy Bonds.............................. 33,539,512
Annual interest charge................................... 7,462,280

This company is a consolidation of the Union Pacific, the Kansas Pacific and the Denver Pacific, effected January 24, 1880.

GROSS EARNINGS.

1879...$20,609,615
1880... 25,494,106

RANGE OF PRICES 1880.

	High-est.	Low-est.	Amount sold.
Stock	113¾	80	2,399,093 shares.
Bonds—U. P. 1st	118	108¼	$4,474,000
Land Grant	116¾	110	418,000
Sink. Fund	122¼	114¾	1,056,000
K. P. 1st 1896 C. Cert.	125	113½	308,000
1st Con	105¼	88	10,167,000
Den. Div. A. Cou. Cer.	114	102	4,267,000
" Assented	110	102	3,178,000
K. P. Income No. 16	102	72¾	351,000

WABASH, ST. LOUIS & PACIFIC.

```
Miles of road owned.....  ........................................:...................1,915
   "      "   leased or partly owned..............................  564
```

```
   Total.................................................................2,479
```
Capital stock :
```
   Common...............................................................$23,337,600
   Preferred (7 per cent., not cumulative).......................  22,900,000
```
```
                                                                    $46,237,600
   Bonded debt.............................................................$42,094,858
   Annual interest charge........................................  2,657,359
```

The company is a consolidation of the Wabash and the St. Louis, Kansas City & Northern, effected November 1, 1879.

GROSS EARNINGS.

```
1879.........................................................$9,124,139
1880.........................................................12,428,111
```

RANGE OF PRICES 1880.

	Highest.	Lowest.	Amount sold.
Stock—Common.....................	48	26½	1,779,230 shares.
Preferred....................	88⅜	51¼	3,652,471 "
Bonds—General Mortgage...........	98 ·	95	$650,000
1st Ex-Coupon..............	112	107½	110,000
1st St. Louis Division........	111	100	473,000
2d Mortgage.................	110	95	1,321,000
Con. Convertible............	112½	93	1,886,000
New.......................	107¾	92½	189,000
Gt. West. 1st Ex. Coup. 1880.	112½	106½	223,000
" 2nd 1893.........	108½	96⅛	1,785,000
Tol. & Wis. Fd. In. C. Cov...	97	80	201,000

NEW YORK STOCK EXCHANGE,

Range of Prices in 1880.

RAILROAD STOCKS.

	Highest.	Lowest.	Amount sold.
Albany and Susquehanna	120	100	7,517
Atchison, Topeka and Santa Fe	148	134⅜	810
Belleville and South Illinois Pref	60	60	100
Boston and New York Air Line Pref	61¾	37	27,832
Burlington, Cedar Rapids and Northern	80⅛	50	39,928
Canada Southern	81⅜	40	819,601
Cedar Falls and Minneapolis	29	14	44,901
Central Iowa	37	25	9,062
" 1st Pref	77½	58	1,256
" 2d Pref	47½	38	1,100
Central of New Jersey	90¼	45	4,743,319
Central Pacific	97½	63	242,361
Chesapeake and Ohio	25¾	15	328,053
" " 1st Pref	36¼	22	53,015
" " 2d Pref	27¼	17	44,779
Chicago and Alton	159½	99½	105,719
" " Pref	160	117	1,077
Chicago, Burlington and Quincy	183½	113	350,325
Chicago, Milwaukee and St. Paul	114¾	66½	5,554,943
" " " Pref	124⅛	99	169,198
Chicago and Northwest	130	87⅛	3,351,898
" " Pref	146½	104	221,154
Chicago, Rock Island and Pacific	204	149	218,770
" " " New	143	100½	
Chicago, St. Louis and New Orleans	48	22	156,718
Chicago, St. Paul and Minneapolis	60½	44¾	110,628
" " " Pref	100	100	144
Chicago, St. Paul, Minn. and Omaha	51	36	410,287
" " " " Pref	101⅜	69	316,190
Cincinnati, Ind., St. Louis and Chicago	89⅛	75	2,242
Cleveland, Columbus, Cincinnati and Ind	96½	61	266,392
Cleveland and Pittsburg Guaranteed	129½	106¾	38,288
Columbus, Chicago and Indiana Central	25⅛	9½	674,525
Danbury and Norwalk	53	50	112
Delaware and Hudson	92¾	60	1,012,069
Delaware, Lackawanna and Western	110¼	68½	8,308,704
Denver and Rio Grande	86½	61⅛	402,383
Dubuque and Sioux City	83	60	3,578
Frankfort and Kokomo	36	20	700
Hannibal and St. Joseph	50⅞	22⅞	1,341,980
" " Pref	105	63½	1,043,237
Harlem	200	158	3,081
Houston and Texas Central	91½	48¾	254,705
Illinois Central	127⅝	99½	322,134

Indiana, Bloomington and Western	52	25	70,823
Indiana, Cincinnati and Lafayette	8	31½	53,120
International and Great Northern	50½	37½	6,038
Kansas Pacific	108	87	27,704
Keokuk and Des Moines	20½	9	4,739
"　　　" Pref	43½	25	2,732
Lake Erie and Western	42¾	20½	781,946
Lake Shore and Michigan Southern	139⅝	95	5,428,252
Long Island	24	20	......
Louisville and Nashville	174	77	346,202
Louisville, New Albany and Chicago	109	80	17,502
Manhattan Elevated	57½	21	1,677,534
Manhattan Beach	50	30	5,897
Marietta and Cincinnati 1st Pref	18	3¾	365,036
"　　　" 2d Pref	12½	2½	109,073
Memphis and Charleston	43	29½	9,912
Metropolitan Elevated	121	83	145,712
Michigan Central	130¼	75	1,412,160
Missouri, Kansas and Texas	49½	28½	3,764,881
Mobile and Ohio	29½	12	183,933
Morris and Essex	123	100	225,550
Nashville, Chattanooga and St. Louis	128	47½	1,615,004
New York Central and Hudson River	155⅜	122	1,756,893
New York Elevated	127¼	109	56,380
New York, Lake Erie and Western	51¼	30	14,307,057
"　　　"　　" Pref	93½	47	603,274
New York, New Haven and Hartford	180	155	6,808
New York, Ontario and Western	32½	20	1,969,564
"　　　"　　" Pref	85⅝	70	1,864
Northern Pacific	38	20	435,152
"　　　" Pref	67½	39⅜	759,090
Ohio Central	28½	14	124,244
Ohio and Mississippi	44½	23	2,973,569
"　　　" Pref	102	57¾	137,655
Panama	225	168	7,690
Peoria, Decatur and Evansville	28½	18	92,037
Philadelphia and Reading	72⅜	13½	2,402,650
Pittsburg, Fort Wayne and Chicago	129	112	5,481
Pittsburg, Titusville and Buffalo	36	30¾	27,300
Rensselaer and Saratoga	129	111	2,821
Rome, Watertown and Ogdensburg	35	19⅞	15,284
St. Louis, Alton and Terre Haute	42	15	70,639
"　　　"　　" Pref	112	42½	88,587
St. Louis, Iron Mountain and Southern	66	34½	2,084,270
St. Louis and San Francisco	48	25¾	151,061
"　　　" Pref	65	33	218,974
"　　　" 1st Pref	100	60	78,709
St. Paul and Duluth	40	25	6,232
"　　　" Pref	79¼	50	2,792
St. Paul, Minneapolis and Manitoba	88	67	10,250
St. Paul and Sioux City	45½	34	123,408
"　　　" Pref	83¼	68	85,251
Stonington	130	129	200
Texas and Pacific	47⅜	30	6,334
"　　　" Trust Certificates	27	25	60,825
Union Pacific	113¾	80	2,309,093
United Companies of New Jersey	180	157½	539
Wabash, St. Louis and Pacific	48	26½	1,779,230
"　　　"　　" Pref	85⅜	51¼	3,652,471
Warren	101½	100	543

TELEGRAPH STOCKS.

	Highest.	Lowest.	Amount sold
American District	81	50	244,437
American Union	75	57⅛	31,391
Atlantic and Pacific	53⅛	32	292,771
Western Union	116⅛	77⅛	5,970,683

EXPRESS COMPANIES.

	Highest.	Lowest.	Amount sold.
Adams	122	106½	13,652
American	66¾	54	44,965
United States	55	42	25,050
Wells, Fargo & Co	113	100	14,717

COAL COMPANIES.

	Highest.	Lowest.	Amount sold.
American	55	55	50
Colorado Coal and Iron	42½	19⅛	46,929
Consolidation	36¾	28	6,650
Cumberland Coal and Iron	70	23	3,740
Cumberland and Elk Lick	45¼	35½	2,200
Maryland	27	16	10,034
Montauk	85	31	55,925
New Central	35	20	86,712
New York and Straitsville	107	105	13,903
Pennsylvania	225	190	1,336

MINING COMPANIES.

	Highest.	Lowest.	Amount sold.
Amie Con	2½	2	1,050
Caribou Con	6	1¼	32,555
Central Arizona	21½	2	422,271
Climax	3¾	1	105,200
Deadwood	25⅝	11⅛	8,418
Excelsior	25½	6	15,018
Homestake	39	26	10,125
La Plata	9⅛	2	18,550
Leadville	4⅞	1½	11,395
Little Pittsburg	30⅛	1⅜	334,242
Mariposa	4⅜	2½	2,910
" Preferred	3	3	200
Ontario	39¾	30	5,470
Quicksilver	24¼	9	54,039
" Preferred	78½	45	90,276
Silver Cliff	6¾	2¼	32,330
Standard	34	20	179,346
Stormont	4¾	2½	26,732
Sutro Tunnel (per share)	4⅛	⅛	937,279

Miscellaneous Stocks.

	Highest.	Lowest.	Amount sold.
Boston Land	12	9¾	2,805
Boston Water Power	19	6½	34,415
Canton	63	40	8,000
Central of New Jersey Land and Imp.	42	37	737
Jerome Park	89	85	1,991
Manhattan Gas	180	179½	200
New York Gas	104	104	200
New York and Texas Land	30	25	300
Oregon Railway and Navigation	147	102	72,018
Pacific Mail	62	27½	3,878,526
Pullman Palace Car	146	107½	17,341

Railroad Bonds.

	Highest.	Lowest.	Amount sold.
Baltimore & Ohio 1st, P. Br	113	108½	37,000
Boston, Hartford & Erie 1st	60	35	6,593,000
" " guar	57¼	40	79,000
Burlington, Cedar Rapids & Northern 1st	100⅜	88⅜	4,134,300
Min & St. L. 1st	110	100	6,000
1st Iowa Ext	106	102	60,000
Iowa C. & W. 1st	110	110	2,000
Central Iowa 1st	115	94	324,000
Coupon debt certificates	91	65	74,000
Central of N. J. 1st	119	115⅛	257,000
Consol. assented	116	90	3,874,000
Conv. assented	115	96	1,254,000
Adjustment	113	98	847,000
Income	97	72½	2,414,000
L. & W. B. con. gu	113½	112½	11,000
Con. assented	106¼	84¼	6,588,000
Income	86	58	341,000
American Dock and Improvement	124	105¾	182,000
Assented	124	104½	421,000
Ches. & Ohio, Series B, int., d	82½	59½	9,874,000
Currency, int. def	51	35	9,119,500
Chicago & Alton 1st	125	116	57,000
Income	106½	103½	49,000
Sinking Fund	115	106	21,000
Joliet & Chicago 1st	108⅛	105	18,000
Lou. & Mo. River 1st	115	110	60,000
" " 2d	108⅜	100	20,000
St. L., Jack. & Chicago 1st	115¼	111⅝	14,000
Chi., Bur. & Quincy 1st	111	108⅛	377,000
Consol	131¼	118¼	878,000
Sinking Fund	104	100	11,000
Chi. & E. Ill. 1st Sinking Fund cur	105½	96¼	68,000
Income	95	90	94,000
Chi., Mil. & St. P. 1st	135	125	70,000
2d	125	112½	36,000
1st gold	128	111	318,000
La Crosse div	125	111½	383,000

I. and M. Div	127	111	159,000
I. and D. Div	124	109	98,000
H. and D. Div	120	107⅛	973,000
C. and M. Div	125	113	326,000
Consol. Sinking Fund	127	107⅞	3,124,000
2d	106	104½	16,000
1st, I. and D. Extension	123⅓	107⅞	962,000
1st, S. W. Div	110½	100	119,000
La C. and Dav. Div	102½	89½	562,000
South Minn. Div	111	100	1,782,000
Chi. and Pac. Div	109¾	106½	55,000
Chicago and Northwest Sinking Fund	112½	107	644,000
Interest	109	104	29,000
Consol	135½	121	585,000
Extension	109	109	12,000
1st	112	106	149,000
Gold, coup	130	115	1,458,000
Gold, reg	127	115	374,000
Sinking Fund, coup	111	106 }	5,000
" " reg	108	107 }	
Iowa Mid. 1st	122	120	15,000
Galena and Chicago Exten	105	103	62,000
Peninsula, 1st conv	126	120	6,000
Chicago and Milwaukee 1st	122½	114	17,000
Winona and St. Paul 1st	111	108	170,000
2d	115	112	36,000
Chicago, Rock Island and Pacific coup	1[illegible]	113½	313,000
Registered	125½	116	239,000
Keo. and Des M. 1st	103	94	196,000
C., St. L. and N. O. 1st con	114	105	24,000
2d income	85	70	46,000
C., St. P. M. and O. cons	106½	98	1,252,000
Chicago, St. P. and M. 1st	109⅝	101½	356,500
Land Grant Income	121	93	337,000
No. Wisconsin 1st	106⅛	91	21,000
St. Paul and Sioux City 1st	110¾	96¾	2,259,000
C., I., St. L. and Chicago con	106	94½	8,000
Cin. and S. 1st, C., C. C. and I	116	103	136,000
1st, Lake Shore	115	107¼	64,000
Cleve., Col., Cin. and Indianapolis 1st	127	117	38,000
Consol. guar	120	107	387,000
Delaware and Hudson 1st, 1884	108⅛	102½	141,000
1st 1891	115	105 }	279,000
1st Extended	106	106 }	
Coupon 1894	117½	107	174,000
Registered 1894	117½	107¾	113,000
Pennsylvania Division Coup	122	110¼	467,000
do. do. Reg	120	111	114,000
Albany and Susquehanna 1st	117	112½	43,000
do. do. 2d	111	107½	145,000
1st Consol. guar	125½	107¼	490,000
Rens. and Saratoga 1st coup	140	124	47,000
1st Registered	137½	125	16,000
Del., Lack. and Western 2d	104¾	100⅝	56,000
Convertible	114½	114½ }	71,000
1907	125	116½ }	
Syracuse, Binghamton and N. Y. 1st	120	113	195,000
Morris and Essex 1st	135	125	116,000
2d	117¾	112	89,000
1900	104¾	103	7,000

Construction	109	99½	26,000
1871	117¼	107½	102,000
1st Consol. guar	125½	107	921,000
Denver and Rio Grande 1st	116	96	6,991,000
1st Consol	116¾	90¾	6,264,000
Denver, South Park and P. 1st	111	104¾	840,000
East Tennessee, Virginia and Georgia 1st	115⅛	104	57,000
Erie, 1st Extended	128	119¾	116,000
2d	109½	103½	105,000
3d	109½	105	153,000
4th	107¾	101	281,000
5th	112¾	109	87,500
1st consol. gold	130½	115½	10,546,000
Long Dock	122	113	95,000
Buffalo, New York and Erie 1st	126	115½	172,000
N. Y., Lake Erie and Western new 2d cons	102⅞	77⅛	172,451,000
1st consol. funded coup	124½	119½	20,000
2d consol. funded coup	98	71	16,171,500
Income	91	67	112,300
Erie and Pitts. consol	105⅝	100	33,000
Frank. and Kokomo	103¾	90	61,000
Galena, H. and H. gold	69	67	27,000
Galena, H. and San A. 1st	103	100	39,000
Hannibal and St. Joseph conv	112½	106	666,000
Houston and Texas Central 1st, main line	113½	106½	332,000
1st Western Div	113	105	116,000
2d con., main line	119	105	599,000
Income and indemnity	99	93	27,000
Ill. Central Dub. & S. C., Cedar F. & M. 1st	113	101	43,000
Ind., Bloom. & Western 1st pref	123	113	20,000
1st	80	69	509,000
2d	70¾	58	495,000
Income	72	42	2,542,000
Ind. Dec. & Sp. 1st	105½	96	558,000
2d	76	60	120,000
International and Great Northern 1st	107	97	623,000
Houston and Great Northern 1st, P. R	106½	93½	58,000
2d purchasing receipts	51½	25	11,000
Int. 2d purchasing receipts	52	25	10,000
2d income	91	65	960,000
Lafayette, Bloomington and Muncie 1st	106	91⅝	1,391,000
Income	74¾	61	443,000
Lake Erie and Western 1st	107¾	93¼	1,331,000
Income	73	53	3,375,909
Lake Shore and Michigan Southern—			
M. S. and N. J. Sinking Fund	112	107½	123,000
Cleveland and Toledo Sinking Fund	112	108	125,000
New	118	107	8,000
Cleveland, Plains. and Ash	118	113¼	2,000
Buffalo and Erie New	123	116½	156,000
Buffalo and State Line	108½	102¾	2,000
Kalamazoo and White Pigeon 1st	113	113	3,000
Detroit, M. and Toledo 1st	121½	115½	12,000
Lake Shore dividend	123	116	21,000
Consol. coup. 1st	133	119	370,000
Consol. reg. 1st	128	118¾	191,000
Consol. coup. 2d	125	114¼	169,000
Consol. reg. 2d	123	115	202,000
Long Island 1st	110¼	107	9,000
Louisville and Nashville con	121	113	248,000

2d gold	106	103	181,000
Cecilian Branch	110½	105	10,000
Nashville and Decatur 1st	115	106½	79,000
N. O. and Mobile Division gd	105½	101½	134,000
General Mortgage	105½	101¼	587,000
Manhattan Beach 1st	110	105	6,000
Marietta and Cincinnati 1st	115	105½	62,000
Metropolitan Elevated 1st	107	98⅝	9,827,000
2d	95	91½	113,000
Michigan Central consol	129	116¾	493,000
1st Sinking Fund	115	106	212,000
Missouri, Kansas and Texas con. assented	117½	92¼	20,458,000
2d income	79	47⅛	59,092,000
Hannibal and Central Missouri 1st	111	108¼	33,000
Mobile and Ohio new	110	95¾	920,000
1st pref. debenture	90	62	6,257,000
2d pref. debenture	58	36	2,034,500
3d pref. debenture	45	28	494,500
4th pref. debenture	44	30	432,000
Nashville, Chattanooga and St. Louis 1st	121	105	339,000
Nevada Central 1st	100	97¼	26,000
N. Y. Central, 1883	107	103	328,000
1887	112½	107	48,000
Real Estate	106	102½	3,000
N. Y. Central and Hudson 1st coupon	137	123¼	648,000
1st registered	135	124	505,000
Hudson River 2d, Sinking Fund	113	109½	51,000
Canada Southern 1st guar	104½	88	7,844,000
Harlem 1st, coupon	134	123½	120,000
1st registered	133	124½	186,000
N. Y. Elevated 1st	120	108½	2,201,000
N. Y. and Texas Land Scrip	27	20	100,500
Ohio Central 1st	107	88¼	2,391,000
Income	60⅛	44	3,395,000
1st, ter. trust	102¾	99½	131,000
Ohio and Mississippi Sinking Fund	122	110	263,000
Consol	120	111	78,000
2d Consol	122½	107½	930,000
1st, Springfield Division	119¼	69	556,000
Oregon River and Navigation 1st	109	89⅝	2,839,000
Pacific Railroads—			
Central Pacific Gold	118	108¼	1,207,000
San Joaquin Branch	109	101¾	203,000
Cal. and Oregon	106½	100	163,000
State Aid	105½	105	28,000
Land Grant	106½	102¾	142,000
Western Pacific	114	103¼	235,000
Missouri Pacific Consol	105	105	40,000
Pacific of Missouri 1st	111	104¾	921,000
2d	117½	106	99,000
St. Louis and San Francisco 2d, Class A	100	87¼	556,000
Class B	89⅞	68	932,000
Class C	87	65	1,087,000
Equipment	104¾	100	293,000
South Pacific of Missouri 1st	106½	100	100,500
South Pacific of California 1st	103¼	96	1,974,000
Texas and Pacific 1st	108	103	17,000
Consol	102	89	200,000
Land Grant, registered	90	56	12,206,000
Rio Grande Division	100	80	5,318,000

Union Pacific 1st	118	108¼	4,474,000
Land Grant	116¼	110	418,000
Sinking Fund	122¼	114¾	1,056,000
Registered	119⅛	115¼	2,000
Col. Trust	107⅜	102	53,000
Kansas Pacific.—			
1st coupon certificates, F. and A.	120	117	47,000
coupon certificates, J. and D.	126	111¼	308,000
Leavenworth Branch	140	100	12,000
Income No. 16	102	72¾	351,000
Denver Division assented, coupon certif	114½	102	4,267,000
Denver Division, ex-coupon	106½	95½	3,178,000
1st consolidated	105¼	88	10,167,000
Pennsylvania.—			
Pittsburg, Fort Wayne and Chicago 1st	140	125	104,500
2d	130½	122½	130,000
3d	121	117½	68,000
Cleveland and Pittsburg consol. S. F.	121½	118	267,000
4th	113	108	17,000
Col., Chi. and Ind. Central 1st consol	110	79½	2,468,000
2d	52	52	1,000
1st, Trust Certificates, assented	106½	78 }	14,282,000
1st, Supplementary	107⅜	78 }	
Income	60	29	9,481,000
Peoria, Decatur and Evansville 1st	107	92	748,000
Income	76	50	785,000
Income, Ev. Division	70	66	65,000
Rome, Watertown and Ogdensburg consol	81½	54	7,850,000
St. Louis, Alton and Terre Haute 1st	115	111	35,500
2d preferred	109	100¼	106,000
2d income	100	89¼	306,500
Belleville and South. Illinois 1st	120	115	2,000
St. Louis and Iron Mountain 1st	119	113	386,000
2d	110	97	3,961,000
Arkansas Branch	110¾	99½	355,000
Cairo and Fulton 1st	115	101	1,324,000
Cairo, Arkansas and Texas	109	97½	631,000
1st pref. income, interest ac	96½	75	4,693,000
2d pref. income, interest ac	87	65½	11,324,000
St. Louis, Vicksburg and Terre Haute 1st gd	120	113	18,000
St. P., Min. and M. 1st	114¼	106⅛	109,000
2d	102	95	66,000
South Side (L. I.) 1st	104	104	6,000
Texas and St. Louis	96⅜	92⅞	341,000
Tol., Peoria and Warsaw, P. C. R. 1st, E. D.	135	123	67,000
Pur. Com. Receipts 1st, West. Div.	142½	123	48,000
Wabash, St. Louis and Pacific, Gen. Mort.	98	95	650,000
Wabash 1879	107¼	91	34,000
Toledo and Warsaw 1st exten	114	107½	110,000
St. Louis Division	111	100	473,000
2d Extended	110	95	1,321,000
Equipment	45	35	35,000
Consol. convertible	112½	93	1,886,000
Great Western 1st	112⅜	106½	223,000
2d	109	96⅛	1,785,000
Quincy and Toledo 1st	108	102½	31,000
Illinois and South. Iowa 1st	101	100	68,500
Wabash Funded Interest—			
Decatur and East St. Louis	98	86	2,000
Quincy and Toledo	98	95	3,500

Toledo and Wabash 2d.................... 98	83	18,000
Wabash and Warsaw 2d.................. 96¾	90	201,000
Great Western 2d........................ 96½	85	48,500
Consol. convertible....................... 97	80	21,000
St. L., Kan. City and North. Real Estate...113	105	602,000
Omaha Division.......................120	106¾	692,000
St. Charles Bridge.......................110	108	352,000
Clarinda Branch.........................102¼	90	93,000
North Missouri 1st.......................123	112	300,000
Western Union Telegraph coupon.............120	113	61,000
Registered.................................117½	113	33,000

NEW YORK STOCK EXCHANGE.

Deliveries of stock may be made either by transfer or by certificates assigned in blank.

Stocks are bought and sold either "cash," "regular way" or on "options," not longer than 60 days.

In "cash" sales the stock is deliverable on the day the sale is made. In "regular way" the stock is deliverable on the following day. A seller's option permits the seller to deliver the stock at any time before the maturing of the contract ; and a buyer's option permits the buyer to demand the stock at any time within the time limited.

In options over three days six per cent. interest is charged to the buyer, and one day's notice is required to terminate the option.

Powers of attorney, or substitution, signed by trustees, guardians, infants, executors, administrators or attorneys are not a good delivery.

When transfer books are closed powers of attorney must be acknowledged before a notary public. A detached power of attorney or of substitution must be similarly acknowledged.

Certificates of stock in the name of a person not a member of the Exchange must be witnessed or guaranteed by a member.

Certificates in the name of an institution, or an officer thereof, must have the assignment or power acknowledged before a notary.

Certificates in the name of a deceased member, or of a firm no longer existing, are a good delivery only while the transfer books are closed.

Whenever a definite name is written upon a bond it is regarded as implying ownership, and must be released and acknowledged before a notary.

A delivery of coupon bonds must be in denominations of $1,000, or $500 ; of registered bonds in sums not exceeding $10,000.

All deliveries of stocks must be made before 2.15 P. M., in default of which the buyer can notify the Vice-President of the Exchange, who will buy in the stock. Similarly, buyers of stock must be prepared to receive, or have the stock sold out for their account.

Before a security can be dealt in it must have been examined and passed on by the Committee on Securities.

Applications to list a stock must be accompanied by a statement of the assets and liabilities of the company, the names of the officers and directors, and the amount of stock or bonds.

All certificates of stock must be printed from plates engraved on steel.

Every company whose stock is listed must have an office in New York City for the transfer and register of its stock.

"PUT."

NEW YORK,....................18

FOR VALUE RECEIVED, the Bearer may DELIVER ME ....Shares of the............................ ....Stock of the
....Company,
at..per cent., any time
in....................days from date.

The undersigned is entitled to all dividends or extra dividends declared during the time.

Expires....................18
............M.

"CALL."

NEW YORK,....................18

FOR VALUE RECEIVED, the Bearer may CALL ON ME
for....................Shares of the............................Stock of the
....Company,
at..per cent., at any time
in........ ....days from date.

The bearer is entitled to all dividends or extra dividends declared during the time.

Expires....................18
............M.

"STRADDLE."

NEW YORK,....................18

FOR VALUE RECEIVED, the bearer may CALL on the undersigned for ....Shares of the
....
at.... ....per cent., any time in
....................days from date.

OR, THE BEARER MAY, at his option, DELIVER the same to the undersigned at........ ....per cent., any time within the period named.

ALL DIVIDENDS OR EXTRA DIVIDENDS declared during the time are to go with the stock in either case, and this instrument is to be surrendered upon the stock being either called or delivered.

Expires....................... ....

NEW YORK MINING STOCK EXCHANGE.

The only contracts and sales allowed are cash and regular bids and offers, and buyer's and seller's option not exceeding 60 days.

Contracts over three days bear interest at 6 per cent. per annum, except when made free of interest, or "flat."

Deliveries must be made before 2.15 P. M. If not so made, after notice to the defaulting party, the contract may be closed under the rule. Such notice must be given not later than 2.30 P. M., or the contract will continue without interest until the following day.

When the transfer books are closed, deliveries may be made by power and certificates in lots of not over 100 shares.

When more than one transfer a day is allowed on the same stock, deliveries shall be made either by transfer or by power and certificate. When only one is allowed, the deliveries must be by power and certificate only, in lots of over 100 shares.

Powers of Attorney, or substitution, signed by trustees, guardians, executors, administrators or attorneys shall not be a good delivery.

Corporations whose stock is dealt in at the Exchange are required to give 30 days' notice, in writing, prior to any increase in their capital stock, or the creation of any mortgage or deed on their property ; and no increased stock shall be a good delivery upon contracts made previous to such notice.

On the day of closing the transfer books of any stock for a dividend, transactions in that stock for *cash* shall be "dividend on" up to the time designated for closing the books. All other transactions will be " dividend off " after 2.15 P. M., or after the closing of the books, should they close before that hour.

When a dividend is declared on a security during the pendency of a contract, the buyer is entitled to the dividend.

AMERICAN MINING STOCK EXCHANGE.

The rules of this Exchange are the same as those at the New York Mining Stock Exchange, excepting such changes as are here noted.

Deliveries must be made to the Clearing House of the Mining Trust Company before 1 o'clock P. M. In case of failure 15 minutes after that time, the contract may be closed under the rule by giving notice in writing delivered at the office of the defaulting broker not later than 1.30 o'clock P. M.

In all sales of stocks the buyer shall pay any assessment levied and not delinquent at the time of sale, provided that the levying of the assessment has been previously announced in open Exchange ; but no assessment, whether payable instanter or otherwise, shall be considered delinquent until *thirty* days from the day on which it was levied.

On all time sales of stock after an assessment becomes delinquent and is thereafter rescinded, the buyer may deduct the amount of the assessment from the contract price of the stock.

MINING STOCKS.

Prices at the New York and American Mining Exchanges in 1880.

	Highest.	Lowest.		Highest.	Lowest.
Alice	7.00	5.88	Iron Silver	5.13	2.65
Alta	5.25	2.20	Julia	3.00	1.50
Alta Montana	1.30	.98	Kings Mountain	1.00	.53
American Flag	.63	.20	Kossuth	.28	.13
Amie	2.40	.36	La Crosse	.59	.12
Argenta	.55	.13	La Plata	9.00	4.00
Atlantic Copper	29.00	19.00	Leadville	4.60	.25
Bassic	18.88	7.38	Leeds	.55	.05
Bechtel	2.50	.80	Leopard	.10	.09
Belcher	10.63	1.85	Leviathan	.45	.04
Belle Isle	1.80	.35	Little Chief	11.50	.61
Belvidere	4.25	1.00	Little Pittsburg	30.13	1.75
Best & Belcher	13.50	8.00	Lucerne	.22	.10
Bodie	11.50	3.00	Mariposa	4.00	.10
Bonanza Chief	.35	.18	Mariposa Preferred	5.00	.30
Boston Con	3.00	.63	Martin White	1.40	.30
Boulder Con	.95	.30	May Belle	.53	.10
Buckeye	.63	.12	Mexican	15.00	6.00
Bull Domingo	8.13	4.00	Mono	8.50	.60
Bullion	2.50	1.30	Moose	3.05	.25
Bulwer	12.50	1.00	Navajo	1.10	.20
Calaveras	2.25	.20	N. Y. & Colorado	2.30	1.25
Caledonia	4.00	1.85	North Belle Isle	.55	.31
California	4.65	1.50	Northern Belle	9.50	.35
Caribou	6.00	1.25	North Standard	2.15	.30
Central Arizona	18.50	4.13	Ontario	39.25	30.00
Cherokee	2.00	1.45	Ophir	10.50	6.50
Chrysolite	23.00	3.50	Original Keystone	1.30	.10
Climax	3.63	.34	Plumas	2.70	1.00
Con. Imperial	.98	.09	Quicksilver	24.13	9.50
Con. Pacific	5.25	.60	Quicksilver Preferred	78.00	45.00
Con. Virginia	5.13	2.05	Rappahannock	.45	.10
Copper Knob	.85	.05	Raymond & Ely	.75	.20
Crown Point	4.00	.77	Red Elephant	.95	.30
Dahlonega	.22	.07	Rising Sun	2.00	1.65
Deadwood	25.00	11.50	Robinson Con	10.13	8.50
Dunderberg	1.85	.50	Savage	3.50	2.00
Dunkin	1.60	1.50	Shamrock	1.30	.80
Durango	.65	.10	Sierra Nevada	27.00	7.00
Eureka Con	22.00	13.75	Silver Cliff	6.25	1.85
Excelsior	25.50	6.00	Silver Islet	54.75	36.88
Exchequer	1.50	1.50	Silver King	14.38	4.50
Father De Smet	9.00	5.00	Silver Nugget	2.05	.09
Findley	.68	.15	South Bodie	.86	.02
Gold Placer	1.90	.25	South Bulwer	2.60	.07
Gold Stripe	2.70	2.05	South Noonday	1.70	1.70
Goodshaw	3.20	.16	Spring Valley	5.25	2.60
Grand Prize	2.00	.70	Standard	38.88	20.00
Granville	.48	.05	Sutro Tunnel	4.13	.70
Great Eastern	.74	.20	Tioga	3.50	.38
Green Mountain	5.00	2.05	Tip Top	6.50	1.75
Hale & Norcross	5.00	2.00	Tuscarora	.44	.08
Homestake	38.00	27.00	Unadilla	.19	.09
Horn Silver	18.50	10.00	Union Con	49.00	8.00
Hukill	5.13	1.10	Willshire	.97	.82
Independence	1.50	.15			

NEW YORK PRODUCE EXCHANGE.

MESS PORK.—Notice in writing must be given three days before delivery, and must be for 250 bbls. Warehouse receipts must be delivered to the first receiver before 11 A. M., and may be transferred until 2:30 P. M. Notice must be given to the last receiver before 4 P. M. of the same day, except on Saturdays, between June 1 and September 30, when transfers shall cease at 2 P. M.

LARD.—Deliveries must be made in lots of 250 tierces, the standard net weight of a tierce being 320 lbs. On contracts, 3 days' written notice, exclusive of Sundays and legal holidays, must be given. A "transferable order" must be issued to the first receiver before 12 M. of the day the notice is given, which must be endorsed by him, and may be transferred until 12 M. of the next business day after its issue. It must be presented by the last receiver to the drawer before 1 P. M. of that day, and the drawer must deliver to the last receiver sampling lots before 3 P. M.

GRAIN.—Deliveries on contracts for 8,000 bushels or over shall be made in lots of 8,000 bushels, and on contracts for 10,000 bushels or over in lots of 10,000 bushels. On deliveries on time contracts the seller must issue a transferable order, drawn on himself, before 12:30 P. M., and such order may be passed to subsequent buyers up to 2:30 P. M., except upon the day of maturity of contract, when the notice shall be good delivery only up to 1:30 P. M., provided that no one shall hold it over 15 minutes. The transferable order must be presented by the last receiver to the drawer before 4 P. M. of the day issued, and the drawer must, on presentation, deliver to the last receiver a specific order for the grain named.

BUTTER.—All natural products of the dairy shall be known as "Butter," all others not the exclusive product of the dairy as "Imitation Butter." When butter is sold "to arrive," it must be accepted or rejected within 24 hours after notice of arrival, between November 1 and April, and within six business hours after, between May 1 and October 1. Butter sold "as are" must be taken with all faults. Members may make such special contracts as they may desire.

NAVAL STORES.—Contracts for future delivery, other than sales "to arrive," or for specific dates, shall be understood to require five days' notice for delivery, but in the absence of such notice a tender of the goods must be made between 10 A. M. and 3 P. M. of the last day specified in the contract. In transactions where quantity is not specified, not less than 25 barrels spirits turpentine, or 100 barrels rosin or tar, shall constitute a good delivery.

PETROLEUM.—On option contracts, when not otherwise stipulated, ten days' notice shall be given, five of which shall be within the delivery time specified. When the term "flat" is used, no notice will be required. Deliveries must be made before 5 P. M., and original deliveries from warehouse or refinery before 4 P. M. Delivery orders may be transferred, provided the receiver does not hold the order more than 15 minutes. All settlements of contracts for Refined Petroleum and Naphtha shall be on the basis of 50 gallons in barrels, and of 45 gallons in bulk, and for Crude Petroleum on the basis of 48 gallons in barrels, and 42 gallons in bulk,

GRAIN CONTRACT.

NEW YORK,....................18

In consideration of one dollar in hand paid, the receipt of which is hereby acknowledged........have this day SOLD TO (OR BOUGHT FROM)..................
...........bushels of.......................New York Inspection, at.........cents per bushel.........deliverable at seller's (or buyer's) option............18 .

This contract is made in view of, and in all respects subject to the By-Laws and Rules established by the New York Produce Exchange, in force at this date.

....

TRANSFERABLE ORDER.

NEW YORK,....................18

M.......................................

Deliver to the order of M........................on........ Contract Sale to.......................dated.................18....at........cents per bushel
....................bushels....................which is to be received by the last endorser hereon, who must pay.........for the same at the rate of.........cents per bushel, cash, except as provided in Rule 19 of the Grain Rules.

....

NEW YORK,....................18

In consideration of one dollar paid by the drawer of the above order to each receiver thereof, the receipt of which is hereby acknowledged, we will, before 4 P. M. this day, present the said order to THE PARTY ISSUING THE SAME, and receive therefor a specific order, and pay for the grain delivered thereon at the rate of....cents per bushel.

It is further agreed that each receiver of this order shall continue his or their liability to each other for the fulfilment of the contracts referred to, until the above grain is delivered and paid for.

Received................M.   ....

NEW YORK,....................18

................accept the above Order from M............................... with all the conditions and obligations thereof, on account of Contract purchase from...........................dated.................18....at........cents per bushel....................paying....................Dollars, to make the price equal to........cents per bushel, which is the price to be paid to the party issuing the order.

Received................M.   ....

LARD CONTRACT.

NEW YORK,....................18

In consideration of one dollar in hand paid, the receipt of which is hereby acknowledged, we have this day sold to (or bought from)........................
Two hundred and fifty tierces Prime Lard, at.............cents per lb., deliverable at seller's (or buyer's) option............................

This contract is made in view of, and in all respects subject to the By-Laws and Rules established by the New York Produce Exchange, in force at this date.

TRANSFERABLE ORDER.

NEW YORK,....................18

Messrs. A. B. & Co. :

On the.......................18....deliver to the order of C. D. & Co., in fulfillment of our contract sale to.......................dated..............:
18 ...at........cents per pound, Two hundred and fifty tierces of Lard, which is to be received by the last endorser hereon, who must pay us for the same at the rate of........cents per pound.   (Signed)   A. B. & Co.

FORM OF ENDORSEMENT.

In consideration of one dollar paid to each receiver of the within order by A. B. & Co., the receipt of which is hereby acknowledged, we will, before 1 P. M. on the ....18....present the within Order to A. B. & Co., and receive from them specific sampling orders, and will receive and pay A. B. & Co. for the Lard delivered thereon at the rate of........cents per pound.

It is further agreed that each receiver of this Order shall continue his or their liability to each other for the fulfillment of the contracts referred to, until the Lard is delivered and paid for. (Signed) C. D. & Co.

New York,...................18....

FORM OF TRANSFER.

We accept the within Order from C. D. & Co., with all the conditions and obligations thereof, on account of contract purchase from them dated.............. 18....at........cents per pound, paying...............dollars to make the price equal to........cents per pound, the price to be paid to A. B. & Co.

(Signed) E. F. & Co.

New York,...................18....

NEW YORK COTTON EXCHANGE.

Contracts for the future delivery of cotton are made for 45,000 pounds or 100 square bales each, deliverable in lots of not less than 50 bales, within the time prescribed in the contract, upon five days' notice to the buyer.

Notice of delivery must be given to the buyer before 10 A. M. of the fifth day prior to the delivery. The party receiving the notice may transfer it to a subsequent party, and it may be given from one transferee to another. Each transfer must be made within 20 minutes, and every person receiving the notice shall endorse upon it the time he receives it.

All notices must be for 45,000 or 22,500 pounds.

Any member to whom cotton is due must accept the transfer when tendered in time, the price being made equal to the price of the contract on which the tender is made; provided the transfer is otherwise in accordance with such contract.

All orders from warehouse or other place of delivery, upon which 5 days' notice has been given, must be delivered to the first receiver before 12 M. of the day before the cotton is due.

When no notice of the delivery is given under the contract, the delivery must be made on the last day stipulated in the contract. The party delivering must, however, present to the first receiver a transferable notice before 11 A. M. of the business day next before that of delivery. Transfers may be made the same as in the case of the five days' notice, and the party with whom the transfer may lodge at 3 P. M. of that day must present it to the drawer before 4 P. M., and receive a warehouse order for the cotton.

Payment for cotton delivered on time contracts is to be made on the day following delivery, except where payment on delivery is required when it is to be made simultaneously with the delivery, notice to that effect having been endorsed on the warehouse order.

The rates of brokerage are as follows : Upon all sales of spot cotton 25 cents per bale to be paid by both buyer and seller.

Upon contracts for future delivery and settlement of the same, 12½ cents on contracts and 6¼ cents for settlements, to be paid by the party employing the broker.

Offers to buy or sell for future delivery in the Exchange must be free of brokerage unless otherwise stipulated.

Upon delivery of cotton upon contracts an additional brokerage of 12½ cents per bale shall be paid by each party delivering or receiving the same.

There are three public calls for cotton contracts daily : at 10.30 A. M., 12 M., and 2. P. M., except on Saturdays, when there are two calls : at 10.30 A. M. and 12.30 P. M.

Contracts falling due on holidays shall be completed on the preceding day, and when a notice of five days is required, it must be given at least 5 days previous to the day preceding such holiday.

When the fifth day previous to the date of delivery falls on a holiday, the transferable order must be issued on the preceding day.

When the day of delivery falls on the day following a holiday, the circulation of transferable and warehouse orders must terminate on the next preceding business day.

FORMS.

No.....   CONTRACT A.

Office of........................

NEW YORK,.........................188

Bought for M.........................   Of.........................

45,000 lbs in about one hundred square bales Cotton, growth of the United States, deliverable from licensed Warehouse in the Port of New York, between the First and Last day of..............next, inclusive. The delivery within such time to be at seller's option, in lots of not less than fifty bales upon five days' notice to buyers. The Cotton to be of any grade from Strict Ordinary to Fair, inclusive, and if Stained not below Strict Good Ordinary, at the price of............ ( )cents per pound for Middling, with additions or deductions for other grades, according to the rates of the New York Cotton Exchange on afternoon of the fifth day previous to the date of the Warehouse Order.

Either party to have the right to call for a margin, as the variations of the market for like deliveries may warrant. And which margin shall be kept good.

This Contract is made in view of, and in all respects subject to, the rules and conditions established by the New York Cotton Exchange, and in full accordance with Article II., Title IV., Chapter Second of the By-Laws.

Respectfully,

....
Per..:...................

For and in consideration of One Dollar to....in hand paid, receipt whereof is hereby acknowledged........accept this Contract with all its obligations and conditions.

TRANSFERABLE NOTICE.

o'clock NEW YORK, 188

To *C. & Co.:*

Take notice that on *we* shall deliver you 45,000 pounds in about one hundred square bales Cotton in accordance with the terms of *our* Contract sale to you dated at cents per pound. We pledge *ourselves* to deliver Warehouse Order to the last holder of this notice upon presentation of the same to *us* between the hours of 11 A. M. and 12 M. o'clock of the being the day previous to that of delivery. The Cotton is to be received and held by the last acceptor hereof as custodian for *us* insured for whom it may concern, and subject to *our* order until *we are* paid at the rate of cents per pound.

F. G. & Co.

CONDITIONS.

In consideration of one (1) dollar paid to each of the acceptors, receipt of which is hereby acknowledged, it is agreed that the last acceptor hereof will, between the hours of 11 A. M. and 12 M. o'clock on the day preceding the present the within notice to *F. G. & Co.*, receive the Warehouse Order for the Cotton therein named, and on the following day receive the Cotton and hold the same as Custodian and Agent for the said *F. G. & Co.*, insured for whom it may concern and subject to *their* order until *they are* paid the full amount of cents per pound and to settle with *them* on the basis of Middling, with allowance for variation of grade in accordance with quotations of the New York Cotton Exchange on day of delivery. It is further agreed that each acceptor hereon shall continue his (or their) liability to each other for the fulfillment of the Contracts until this notice shall have been returned to *F. G. & Co.*, and a Warehouse Order specifying the Cotton to be delivered received by the last acceptor hereof from *F. G. & Co.*, at which time all responsibilities of intermediate parties shall cease.

C. & Co.

FORM OF TRANSFER.

o'clock NEW YORK, 188

Messrs. *I. S. & Co.:*

We accept the above with all its conditions and obligations, and you will please take notice that in accordance therewith we shall deliver you 45,000 pounds in about one hundred square bales Cotton on account of *our* Contract sale to you, dated The Cotton to be paid for at the price of transferable notice.

C. & Co.

RANGE OF PRICES IN 1880.

	Uplands		New Orleans		Texas	
	Highest.	Lowest.	Highest.	Lowest.	Highest.	Lowest.
Ordinary	11½	7 15-16	11⅝	7 15-16	11⅝	7 15-16
Strict Ordinary	11⅞	8 9-16	12	8 11-16	12	8 11-16
Good Ordinary	12 5-16	9 9-16	12 7-16	9 11-16	12 7-16	9 11-16
Strict Good Ordin.	12 9-16	9 15-16	12 11-16	10 1-16	12 11-16	10 1-16
Low Middling	12⅞	10 7-16	13	10 11-16	13	10 11-16
Strict Low Middl.	13 1-16	10 11-16	13 3-16	10 15-16	13 3-16	10 15-16
Middling	13¼	10 15-16	13⅜	11 3-16	13⅜	11 3-16
Good Middling	13½	11 5-16	13⅝	11 9-16	13⅝	11 9-16
Strict Good Middl.	13¾	11 9-16	13⅞	11 3-16	13⅞	11 3-16
Middling Fair	14¼	12 1-16	14⅜	12 5-16	14⅜	12 5-16
Fair	15	12 11-16	15⅛	12 15-16	15⅛	12 15-16

STAINED.

	Highest.	Lowest.
Good Ordinary	11 5-16	7⅝
Strict Good Ordinary	12¼	8½
Low Middling	12⅜	9 5-16
Middling	12 13-16	10⅛

AGGREGATE MONTHLY TRANSACTIONS.

	Spot Sales.	Futures Sales.	Futures Deliveries.
January	13,684	3,063,000	32,700
February	19,652	3,079,600	12,700
March	18,371	3,050,000	18,000
April	80,845	4,448,700	26,700
May	38,691	2,094,500	12,700
June	28,470	1,391,500	11,400
July	15,224	1,191,000	10,200
August	23,369	1,615,700	18,500
September	26,710	2,706,100	35,800
October	33,285	2,161,700	20,600
November	28,077	3,443,700	11,800
December	24,120	3,178,500	18,600
Total	350,498	31,424,000	229,700

NEW YORK PETROLEUM EXCHANGE.

A *delivery* of crude oil is made by tendering the purchaser an accepted order or certificate on the pipe line named in the transaction.

A *spot delivery* must be made before 2 P. M. on the day the transaction occurs, unless the purchase is made after 2 P. M., when the delivery must be made before 2 P. M. on the next business day.

A *regular delivery* is made during banking hours on or before the third business day after the transaction.

A *seller's option* gives the seller the privilege of terminating a contract any time within the time specified in the contract. If the oil is tendered before 2 P. M. it must be accepted on the same day ; if after 2 P. M., not until 10 A. M. the next day. If the contract runs to maturity, the oil must be delivered before the expiration of banking hours on that day.

A *buyer's option* permits the buyer to terminate the contract at any time within the time specified by the contract. To ensure delivery on date of demand, the demand must be made before 12 o'clock noon ; if made after that hour, the oil must be delivered before 12 o'clock noon of the next business day. If no demand is made the buyer must receive the oil on the day the contract matures, before expiration of banking hours.

Options with notice give the buyer or seller respectively the right to terminate a contract before maturity, by presenting the notice agreed upon. After notice is given the contract matures before 3 o'clock on the same day.

In all contracts in which the term "about " is used, either as to time or quantity, the variation shall n**o**t exceed 10 per cent. in quantity, or the time three days.

In public offers to buy or sell, no amount or kind of oil being mentioned, the amount will be considered to be 1,000 barrels, and the kind United Pipe Line Certificates.

FORM OF ORDER.

Acceptance.   This Order not good until accepted.

No........ 18

THE   UNITED   PIPE   LINES

Incorporated March 28, 1877.

Deliver to..or order

..................................Barrels Crude Petroleum (of 42 gallons each),

and charge to account of..

IT IS AGREED, that the Petroleum mentioned in this order, is held by the United Pipe Lines, subject to a transportation charge of twenty (20) cents per Barrel, and a storage of five-eights of one cent per Barrel for each fifteen days or fractional part thereof, from and after date of issue.

IT IS FURTHER AGREED, that this order shall be returned to the United Pipe Lines for exchange in six months from date of issue, or be subject to a storage charge of one-third of one cent per Barrel daily thereafter until returned.

IT IS FURTHER AGREED, that the United Pipe Lines shall not, in any event, be liable for any loss of Crude Petroleum resulting from lightning, fire, storms, or other unavoidable causes, it being distinctly understood and agreed, that any such loss or losses shall be charged pro rata upon all the Petroleum in their custody at the time of such loss or destruction, and that the quantity of Petroleum called for by this order shall be reduced by its proportion of such loss or destruction.

AND IT IS FURTHER AGREED, that transportation and all accrued storage charges shall be paid on the amount so deducted.

Order₋No......   ....Bbls., Collect........cents per Bbl.

YEARLY SUMMARY AND RECAPITULATION, 1880.

	January.	February.	March.	April.	May.	June.
Pipe Runs......	67,750	62,952	67,326	68,147	59,176	70,231
Shipments......	52,503	47,707	51,071	27,172	28,439	25,302
Exports........	36,337	25,785	24,635	17,849	15,033	24,726
Charters.......	18,303	22,996	18,954	12,483	18,375	38,843
Stock First of } Month. .... }	8,552,256	8,984,341	9,405,240	9,834,457	11,001,304	11,737,890
Wells Complet.	242	279	367	451	441	331

	July.	August.	September	October.	November.	December.
Pipe Runs..	71,207	71,253	68,032	71,779	67,858	70,062
Shipments..	33,672	43,033	41,180	53,739	40,567	43,097
Exports....	31,646	42,059	35,791	31,973	18,925	24,311
Charters...	35,419	30,270	33,566	17,809	21,746	20,425
St'k 1st of } Month }	12,720,220	13,609,369	14,383,551	15,249,661	15,678,127	16,402,431
Wells Com.	337	397	352	358	350	358

	Pipe Runs.	Shipments.	Exports.	Charters.
Total	24,868,325	15,839,773	9,986,655	8,812,229
Daily Average	67,946	43,276	27,285	24,077
Smallest	59,176	25,302	15,033	12,483
Largest	71,779	53,739	42,059	38,842

Average Price of Crude Petroleum During each Month.

January	110	May	86⅜	September	98 7-16
February	101 9-16	June	107 3-16	October	96⅜
March	90 5-16	July	104 1-16	November	91 9-16
April	78¾	August	91¼	December	94 1-16

Average for Year, 96. Highest, 125. Lowest, 71⅛

Highest and Lowest Prices of Refined During Each Month.

	New York. Highest.	New York. Lowest.	London. Highest.	London. Lowest.	Antwerp. Highest.	Antwerp. Lowest.	Bremen. Highest.	Bremen. Lowest.
January	8⅛	7⅝	6⅝	5¾	20¼	17¾	765	685
February	8	7½	6¼	6	18¾	18	750	715
March	7⅞	7½	6⅛	5¾	19	18⅜	740	720
April	7⅞	7⅜	6⅛	5⅞	19¼	17¾	750	710
May	7⅝	7½	6¼	6	18¼	17½	715	690
June	10½	7⅞	8½	6⅜	22½	18¼	930	720
July	10¼	9	8¼	7½	23½	21½	985	930
August	9⅜	8⅝	8¼	7⅝	23¾	22	950	890
September	11⅞	9⅜	10	8	28¾	23½	1110	930
October	12¼	11¾	10	9¼	28¼	26⅞	1110	1050
November	12	9	9⅞	8⅛	28⅛	23⅝	1065	9
December	10	9	11⅝	8	25⅝	24	940	9

GENERAL STATISTICS.

UNITED STATES.

Debt December 31, 1880.

Interest bearing	$1,675,265,400
Total	2,121,481,475
Total, less cash in Treasury	1,899,181,735

Bonds Outstanding December 31.

6s Currency Registered	$64,623,512
6s 1881	201,556,000
5s 1881	469,651,050
4½s 1891	250,000,000
4s 1907	738,420,400
Total	$1,724,250,962

GOLD AND SILVER.

Stock of gold December 31 .... $486,683,049
" silver " " 163,860,633
Production of gold 1880............................... 33,522,182
" silver " 40,005,364
Exports of gold and silver................................. 16,045,901
Imports " 85,275,723
Excess of imports gold and silver..................... 69,229,822
Gold coined in 1880......................... 62,283,279
Silver " " 27,409,706
Gold certificates outstanding December 31................ 6,582,380
Silver " " " 36,127,711

IMMIGRATION.

1880...586,068

RAILROADS.

Miles constructed in 1880..............................7,150
" foreclosed " 3,775
Debt of foreclosed roads...........................$166,568,000
Capital " " 97,313,700
Earnings of 44 roads.............................. 193,036,245

POPULATION.

1880...50,152,554

FAILURES.

Number...4,735
Liabilities...$65,752,000

FOREIGN TRADE. ·

Exports domestic merchandise....................$875,580,493
" foreign " 14,069,347
Imports " " 696,803,433
Excess of exports............................... 192,846,407

PRODUCTS IN 1880.

Wheat, bushels......................................481,000,000
Cotton, bales..................................... 6,000,000
Iron, tons.. 3,300,000
Coal, anthracite, tons............................ 23,437,242

CURRENCY DECEMBER 31.

Legal tenders outstanding......................... $346,681,016
Trade dollars 10,000,000
Gold coin and bullion (estimated)................. 497,000,000
Standard silver dollars........................... 28,000,000
Gold certificates................................. 6,582,380
Silver " 36,127,711
National bank notes 343,219,943
National gold bank notes.......................... 1,135,260

Total..$1,268,746,310
Amount in banks and Treasury......................$425,928,741
Amount left in circulation........................ 842,817,569

NATIONAL BANKS.

Number September 1...2,072
Capital...$454,215,062
Surplus..120,145,649
Dividends paid, year ended September 1............................36,411,473
Ratio dividends to capital, 6 months..............................4.03 per cent.

NON-DIVIDEND PAYING.

Number, year ended September 1.......................................230
Capital...$28,370,675

CIRCULATION.

Notes outstanding December 31....................................$343,219,943
Gold notes   "   "   " 1,135,260

RESERVE OCTOBER 1, 1880.

Deposits of 2,090 banks..$968,000,000
Reserve required..201,000,000
Reserve held..323,000,000

TAXATION (U. S.) YEAR ENDED JULY 1.

On circulation..$3,153,635
On deposits...4,058,710
On capital..379,424
                                                                _____
    Total...$7,591,770

BONDS TO SECURE CIRCULATION DECEMBER 31.

Currency 6s..$4,019,000
6 per cents...50,719,750
5 per cents...8,330,550
4½ per cents..36,710,450
4 per cents...110,043,800
                                                                _____
    Total...$359,823,550

STATEMENT Showing the Financial and Economic Transactions of the United States of America for the Four Years Ended March 1, 1881.

	For Year Ended March 1, 1878.	For Year Ended March 1, 1879.	For Year Ended March 1, 1880.	For Year Ended March 1, 1881.	TOTAL.
Total receipts	$265,342,831 96	$262,058,817 04	$308,762,742 93	$350,386,715 41	$1,192,551,107 24
Total expenditures	218,280,531 54	235,084,982 91	280,047,064 51	257,323,527 83	990,755,706 03
Total debt, less cash in Treas.	2,042,037,129 08	2,026,207,541 68	1,905,112,221 17	1,879,650,412 77	......
Decrease of debt	40,744,013 96	15,829,587 42	31,095,320 49	115,155,808 40	203,824,730 27
Annual interest charge	92,587,283 50	101,515,647 50	82,211,663 00	76,445,937 50	......
Available cash in Treasury, includ'g resumption fund	72,920,913 38	144,685,042 50	150,031,706 36	160,062,822 20	......
Gold coin & bull. held by Trea.	121,728,854 95	133,265,559 43	146,750,758 04	173,038,253 01	......
Silver coin & bull. held by Trea.	8,454,909 29	35,621,680 28	62,676,711 57	84,104,820 08	......
Exports of live stock	4,205,883 00	10,853,211 00	12,065,459 00	20,681,738 00	47,806,331 00
Exports of other food	260,732,809 00	326,752,030 00	374,568,342 00	454,244,111 00	1,127,317,292 00
Total exports—Merchandise	639,485,209 00	725,854,206 00	767,875,740 00	915,271,563 00	3,048,488,804 00
Specie	47,103,365 00	26,391,143 00	23,922,972 00	16,028,803 00	113,446,283 00
Total imports—Merchandise	175,838,318 00	432,091,123 00	555,560,606 00	703,130,889 00	2,108,642,032 00
Specie	25,200,030 00	26,999,280 00	92,714,238 00	98,570,197 00	243,482,765 00
Product. of cotton...No. bales.	1,485,123	4,811,265	5,073,531	5,761,252	20,131,471
Product. of wool...No. pounds.	207,000,000	211,000,000	232,500,000	261,000,000	914,500,000
Product. of wheat...No. bush.	364,194,146	420,122,400	448,756,630	480,440,723	1,713,922,899
Product. of corn....No. bush.	1,342,558,000	1,388,218,750	1,547,901,790	1,537,585,900	5,816,214,110
Product. of pig iron..No. tons.	2,066,594	2,301,215	2,711,853	3,300,000	10,109,642
Product. of coal....No. tons.	54,308,250	52,130,584	65,808,394	69,200,931	241,448,108

NOTE.—The debt, less cash in the Treasury March 1, 1877, was $2,048,781,143 01, and the annual interest charge, $94,403,645 30; showing a decrease in the debt during the four years, as above, of $204,821,730 27, and of the annual interest charge, $17,957,704.

TREASURY DEPARTMENT, March 1, 1881.

JOHN SHERMAN, Secretary.

NEW YORK STATE.

DEBT, FUNDED.

October 1...$9,122,054

CANALS, 1880.

Tonnage carried...6,462,290
Tolls collected..$1,155,257

BANKS, STATE, OCTOBER 1.

Number...68
Capital..$18,738,290
Deposits.. 61,795,773
Resources... 99,850,755
Surplus... 6,058,280

BANKS, SAVINGS, JULY 1.

Number..128
Resources..$376,211,240
Deposits.. 335,461,570
Surplus... 40,543,454
Number of Depositors......................................912,863

INSURANCE, FIRE.

Number..167
Assets..$143,248,869
Liabilities.. 94,107,073
Cash income (year).. 60,458,160
Cash expenditures (year)................................. 58,822,513

INSURANCE, LIFE, HOME COMPANIES.

Number...12
Assets..$202,562,831
Liabilities... 169,675,366
Surplus... 32,887,465

INSURANCE, LIFE, OTHER STATES.

Number...19
Assets..$198 952,961
Liabilities... 166,562,705
Surplus... 32,390,266

INSURANCE, MARINE.

Number...18
Assets...$20,147,902
Surplus.. 3,565,707

INSURANCE, CASUALTY.

Number 4
Assets $1,800,000
Net Surplus 271,000

FAILURES, 1880.

Number (exclusive of New York City) 461
Liabilities   "   "   " $5,617,766

POPULATION.

1880 5,083,173

NEW YORK CITY.

STOCK EXCHANGE.

Shares of stock sold 1880 97,200,000
Railroad bonds "   " $569,910,000
Government "   "   " 58,460,000
State "   "   " 15,497,400
Shares of city bank stock sold 1880 15,354

MINING EXCHANGES.

New York, shares sold 1880 20,587,570
American,   "   " 8,145,505

DRY GOODS.

Entered for consumption, 1880 ..... $86,914,282
   "   " warehousing   " 23,995,062
Withdrawn from warehouse 25,763,496

CITY DEBT.

Stocks and bonds December 31, 1880 ..... $106,066,240

FAILURES 1880.

Number 415
Amount of liabilities $19,450,744
Amount of assets 8,146,291

POPULATION.

1880 1,206,590

INTEREST.

Average rate on call loans ..... 4.9 per cent.

WEEKLY CLEARINGS OF CITY BANKS.

Jan. 3..$604,197,943	May 1..$697,435,051	Sept. 4.. $603,877,203
" 10.. 657,695,260	" 8.. 790,386,569	" 11.. 625,650,183
" 17.. 787,728,198	" 15.. 867,632,049	" 18.. 623,375,655
" 24.. 743,125,031	" 22.. 759,515,331	" 25.. 573,355,801
" 31.. 772,270,895	" 29.. 795,990,673	Oct. 2.. 705,598,706
Feb. 7.. 720,978,130	June 5.. 639,336,131	" 9.. 651,169,020
" 14.. 683,453,357	" 12.. 737,534,533	" 16.. 693,917,360
" 21.. 795,314,114	" 19.. 616,148,141	" 23.. 872,895,695
" 28.. 725,419,855	" 26.. 607,558,981	" 30.. 785,361,621
Mar. 6.. 895,014,025	July 3.. 711,472,517	Nov. 6.. 866,393,048
" 13.. 827,801,840	" 10.. 452,751,881	" 13.. 896,540,451
" 20.. 748,481,804	" 17.. 560,486,032	" 20.. 868,076,513
" 27.. 644,453,967	" 24.. 625,916,274	" 27..1,072,680,747
April 3.. 771,019,670	" 31.. 586,540,682	Dec. 4..1,155,094,682
" 10.. 810,774,898	Aug. 7.. 644,309,967	" 11.. 940,101,842
" 17.. 849,817,403	" 14.. 551,923,441	" 18.. 974,074,998
" 24.. 720,947,846	" 21.. 480,785,189	" 24.. 804,522,749
	" 28.. 522,899,382	" 31.. 817,931,113

BANK CHANGES IN 1880.

	January 3.	December 31.
Loans	$276,706,200	$297,756,700
Specie	48,282,100	58,047,900
Legal Tenders	12,723,500	12,796,600
Deposits	242,087,100	272,466,900
Circulation	23,748,600	18,408,200
Capital	60,475,200	60,475,200
Clearances	604,197,943	817,931,113

GRAIN MOVEMENTS IN NEW YORK IN 1880.

	Receipts. Bushels.	Exports. Bushels.
Wheat	60,381,021	61,605,886
Corn	60,983,850	49,704,960
Oats	13,978,268	427,794
Barley	3,926,266	254,833
Rye	2,023,155	2,181,183
Flour	24,342,021	18,741,335
Meal	2,301,964	1,640,660
Total grain	145,132,764	114,822,805
Total grain, flour and meal	171,776,749	135,204,800

INTEREST.

BANK OF ENGLAND RATE.

January 1 to June 9	3	per cent.
June 9 to December 1	2½	"
December 1 to December 31	3	"

FOREIGN EXCHANGE.

	60 Days —		Sight —	
	High-est.	Low-est.	High-est.	Low-est.
January	4.83½	4.81½	4.86	4.84
February	4.85	4.82½	4.88	4.85
March	4.86	4.85	4.89	4.88
April	4.86	4.85	4.89	4.87½
May	4.87	4.85½	4.90	4.88½
June	4.87	4.85	4.90	4.87½
July	4.85	4.83	4.87½	4.85
August	4.83	4.82	4.85	4.84
September	4.82	4.81½	4.84½	4.84
October	4.82½	4.81½	4.85	4.84
November	4.82	4.79½	4.81½	4.81½
December	4.81½	4.79	4.81½	4.81½

GOLD AND SILVER.

From the BULLION ANNUAL.

By permission of the *Bullion Publishing Co.*

WORLD'S PRODUCTION AND SUPPLY.

Taking the discovery of America, or the year 1492, as a starting point, we estimate the world's stock of gold at that time at 26,500,000 ounces, of silver at 326,000,000 ounces. Since the year 1492 we have practically accurate accounts of yearly production. Grouping the total between the discovery of America and the discovery of gold in California, or between 1492 and 1848, we find the production of gold was 160,000,000 ounces, and the production of silver was 4,800,000,000 ounces. The yearly production since 1848 is given in the following table :

	Gold, ounces.	Silver, ounces.	Proportion of gold to silver.
1849	1,355,000	31,200,000	1 to 23,025
1850	2,222,500	31,200,000	1 to 14,038
1851	3,380,000	32,000,000	1 to 9,437
1852	6,637,500	32,480,000	1 to 4,893
1853	7,772,500	32,480,000	1 to 4,178
1854	6,372,500	32,480,000	1 to 5,096
1855	6,753,750	32,480,000	1 to 4,778
1856	7,380,000	32,520,000	1 to 4,400
1857	6,663,750	32,520,000	1 to 4,880
1858	6,232,500	32,520,000	1 to 5,217
1859	6,242,500	32,600,000	1 to 5,222
1860	5,962,500	32,640,000	1 to 5,474
1861	5,690,000	34,160,000	1 to 6,000
1862	5,387,500	36,160,000	1 to 6,920
1863	5,347,500	39,360,000	1 to 7,364
1864	5,650,000	41,360,000	1 to 7,285
1865	6,010,000	41,560,000	1 to 6,915
1866	6,055,000	40,580,000	1 to 6,520
1867	5,701,250	43,380,000	1 to 7,608
1868	5,456,250	40,180,000	1 to 7,321
1869	5,311,250	38,000,000	1 to 7,154
1870	5,342,500	41,260,000	1 to 7,723
1871	5,350,000	48,840,000	1 to 9,129
1872	4,980,000	52,200,000	1 to 10,481
1873	4,810,000	71,400,000	1 to 14,843
1874	4,537,500	57,200,000	1 to 12,606
1875	4,875,000	64,400,000	1 to 13,230
1876	4,750,000	59,200,000	1 to 12,463
1877	4,850,000	64,800,000	1 to 13,335
1878	4,325,000	68,800,000	1 to 15,905
1879	5,270,000	64,830,000	1 to 12.310
1880	*4,740,000	58,500,000	1 to 12.325
Total.	171,443,750	2,393,290,000	1 to 13.959

*Estimated.

Following is a summary of the world's production

and supply of gold and silver from the earliest date to January 1, 1881:

	Gold, ounces.	Silver, ounces.
To World's stock in 1492.....	26,000,000	326,000,000
Production 1492 to 1848......	160,000,000	4,800,000,000
" 1849 to 1880......	171,443,750	2,393,290,000
Total..............	357,443 750	7,519,290,000

The stock of gold and silver, had none been lost or destroyed, would therefore amount at this time to 357,443,750 ounces of gold and 7,519,290,000 ounces of silver. Estimating the annual loss from abrasion and total destruction at one-tenth of one per cent. per annum, would make a total since 1492 of 39,-000,000 ounces of gold and 852,000,000 ounces silver lost to the world, leaving the actual supply at the present time as shown in the following table:

	Gold, ounces.	Silver, ounces.
Production........	357,443,750	7,519,290,000
Destroyed........	39,000,000	852,000,000
Present stock...	318,443,750	6,667,290,000

These totals represent the amount of gold and silver of every description in the world at this time, embracing coin, bullion and the metal employed in the arts, which at any time can be converted into coin or bullion.

The amount of gold and silver in circulation and held as reserve in National Treasuries and in banks in the world is estimated as follows:

	Gold, ounces.	Silver, ounces.
Circulation	141,000,000	1,990,000,000
Treasury Reserve	7,700,000	95,500,000
Bank Reserves	21,200,000	260,500,000
Total	169,900,000	2,346,000,000

Deducting the above amounts from the present supply of gold and silver, as shown in the preceding table, and the following result appears:

	Gold, ounces.	Silver, ounces.
Present Stock	318,443,750	6,667,290,000
Circulation and Reserves	169,900,000	2,346,000,000
Balance	148,543,750	4,321,290,000

This balance represents the amount of gold and silver in the world at the present time, existing in the shape of hoardings or employed in the arts, and capable of being converted into money.

The stock of gold and silver in the United States at the close of 1880 was $650,543,682, of which $486,683,049 were gold and $163,860,632 were silver. The report of the mint for the year ended June 30, 1879, showed that the amount of coin outstanding at that date was as follows: Gold, $286,490,698; silver, $112,050,985; total, $398,541,683. The amount coined, less recoinage, during the fiscal year ended June 30, 1880, was: Gold, $55,948,407; silver, $27,903,139; total, $83,851,546, and the net imports during that period were : Gold, $16,519,586 ; silver, $2,-642,896 ; total, $19,162,482. The amount in circulation on June 30, 1880, was therefore $358,958,691 gold and $142,597,020 silver, making a total of $501,-555,711. The amount of bullion held in the mint on June 30, 1880, was $40,724,358 gold and $6,263,613 silver, making a total of $46,987,971. The production of the United States from July 1st to December 31st, 1880, was $18,000,000 gold and $19,000,000 silver, a total of $37,000,000. The net imports of coin and bullion during the last six months of 1880 was $69,000,000 gold, and the net export of silver was $4,000,000, making a net import of gold and silver of $65,000,000. Adding the amount in circulation on June 30, 1880, the bullion held by the mint on that date, the production since and the net imports of coin and bullion, and the stock in the United States appears as follows : Gold, $486,683,049 ; silver, $163,860,633 ; total, $650,543,682.

Of the total production of the world to 1848 the United States contributed 1,000,000 ounces gold, or less than 1 per cent. of the world's supply at that date. Since 1848 the yearly production of gold and silver in the United States was as follows :

	Gold, ounces.	Silver, ounces.		Gold, ounces.	Silver, ounces.
1849..	2,000,000	......	1866..	2,675,000	8,000,000
1850..	2,500,000	......	1867..	2,575,000	10,400,000
1851..	2,750,000	......	1868..	2,400,000	9,600,000
1852..	3,000,000	160,000	1869..	2,475,000	9,600,000
1853..	3,250,000	160,000	1870..	2,500,000	12,800,000
1854..	3,000,000	160,000	1871..	1,794,900	18,288,000
1855..	2,750,000	160,000	1872..	1,972,973	16,422,000
1856..	2,750,000	160,000	1873..	2,022,880	22,681,680
1857..	2,750,000	160,000	1874..	2,005,152	24,398,400
1858..	2,500,000	160,000	1875..	2,087,257	27,235,128
1859..	2,500,000	160,000	1876..	2,216,425	33,205,337
1860..	2,300,000	800,000	1877..	2,225,000	30,400,000
1861..	2,150,000	1,200,000	1878..	1,875,000	28,000,000
1862..	1,950,000	2,400,000	1879..	1,577,000	30,000,000
1863..	2,000,000	5,600,000	1880..	1,626,000	31,200,000
1864..	2,300,000	8,000,000			
1865..	2,650,000	8,800,000	Total..	75,127,587	340,310,545

The above table shows that the production of gold in the United States from 1848 to date aggregated 75,127,587 oz., or 44 per ct. of the world's production during the same period. The production of silver in the United States amounted to 340,310,545 ounces, or 14 per cent. of the world's production.

PRODUCTION OF UNITED STATES IN 1880.

A reference to Table II. Appendix, shows that the production of the United States for 1880, including about $3,000,000 from Mexico and British Columbia, amounted to $80,167,936, a gain of $4,-818,435 over 1879. The production of gold aggregated $33,522,182 in 1880, against $32,539,920 in 1879, and of silver $40,005,364 against $38,623,812,

a gain of nearly $1,000,000 gold and about $1,400,-
000 silver. Colorado leads the list as a producer, showing $21,284,989 to its credit. California follows with
$18,276,166, then Nevada with $15,031,621. Utah
is fourth, showing an output of $6,450,953. Arizona
is fifth, Dakota sixth, Montana seventh, Idaho eighth,
Oregon ninth, New Mexico tenth and Washington
eleventh.

Colorado, the banner State of 1880, presents a very
satisfactory showing. In the past four years it has
risen from fourth to first place. It produced in 1880
$21,284,989, against $14,413,515 in 1879, $6,232,747
in 1878 and $7,913,549 in 1877. Its yield last year
was about 30 per cent. of the entire yield of the
United States; last year it was less than 20 per cent.;
in 1878 it was about 8 per cent., and in 1877 the
ratio was about the same. The increase over 1879
is $6,871,474, which is principally made up by the
increased output of Leadville. The yield amounts
to $15,095,153 against $10,189,521 in 1879, a gain
of nearly $5,000,000.

The total production of Leadville, from 1860 to
the close of 1880 was $35,700,000. The produc-
tion of the several counties of Colorado for 1880,
is placed as follows:

	1879.	1880.
Lake................$11,477,046		$15,095,000
Gilpin............. 2,608,055		2,500,000
Clear Creek......... 1,912.410		2,500,000
Boulder....... 800,000		500,000
Custer............. 720,000		800,000
Park................. 434,749		400,000
Gunnison.....,...... 800,000		200,000
Summit............. 295.717		450 000
Chaffee............. 71,240		100,000
San Juan........... 483,500		300,000

There has been very little variation in the production of California for the past four years, the aggregate never falling below $18,000,000, and never
reaching $19,000,000. Last year the production ag-
gregated $18,276,166, an increase over 1879 of $75,-
193. There was a decrease of about $350,000 in
silver, made up by a gain of about $425,000 in gold.
For the first time California leads Nevada in the
amount of yield, and takes second place.

Nevada's production has fallen off until it is but
little more than one-quarter of what it was in 1877.
Its decline appears as follows :

1877............................	$51,580,290
1878............................	35,181,949
1879............................	21,997,714
1880............................	15,031,621

A decrease is noticed in the two most prominent
districts of the State. The Comstock shows a falling
off from $8,830,562 in 1879 to $5,312,592 in 1880,
a loss of $3,517,970. The production of Eureka
District was only $4,639,025 in 1880, against $5,859,-
269 in 1879, a decrease of $1,220,236. The two
districts show an aggregate loss of over $4,700,000.

Utah has met with encouragement during 1880,
and makes a record of $6,450,953, about $1,000,000
more than in 1879, $400,000 more than in 1878, and
$1,700,000 less than in '77. Salt Lake and Silver Reef
have done much to swell the production of the Terri-

tories, the latter's output being estimated at over $1,-
050,000, an average of nearly $50,000 to each stamp.
Utah is the fourth on the list of producers, a position
which it has occupied for three years. In 1877 it was
the third, leading Colorado, now the first.

Arizona is the fifth on the list of producers, and
its success has been so great that the most extraordinary estimates of its production for 1880 have been
made, as high as from $7,500,000 to $10,000,000 being
claimed. The actual yield may be safely put at not
more than $4,500,000, and these figures seem large
when compared with the previous year, when only
$1,900,000 were realized. Arizona was only the
eighth in order of production in 1879, but last year
she stepped over the heads of Oregon, Idaho and
Dakota.

Dakota, the sixth producer, occupies the same position which it did in 1879. Its production increased
from $3,208,987 to $4,123,081. Montana is the
seventh, and records a yield for 1880 of $3,822,379,
a gain of about $200,000 over 1879. In the latter
year it was fifth in point of production. Idaho has
dropped from the seventh to the eighth place, and
her yield has decreased from $2,091,300 in 1879 to
$1,894,747 in 1880. Oregon maintains its place as
ninth on the list, giving a yield of $1,059,641, a gain
of $21,000 over 1879. New Mexico, the tenth, has

increased its yield from $622,800 to $711,300, and Washington, the eleventh, from $85,330 to $105,-164.

WORLD'S USE OF THE PRECIOUS METALS.

From Table I., Appendix, it appears that only one country, India, uses silver exclusively. Its population amounts to 190,663,623, and the amount of silver in circulation is $1,015,000,000.

The countries using silver as full legal tender, as well as gold, are as follows :

	Population.	Full legal tender Silver.
United States	49,500,000	$72,847,750
Germany	42,727,360	109,480,000
France	36,905,788	540,786,000
Belgium	5,336,185	55,438,000
Switzerland	2,753,854	10,000,000
Italy	27,769,475	20,900,000
Austria	35,904,435	37,000,000
Netherlands	3,579,529	57,600,000
Spain	16,625,869	40,000,000
Mexico	9,276,079	40,000,000
Peru	2,673,075	1,819,933
Central America	2,600,000	373,919
Argentine Republic.	2,000,000	2,000,000
Cuba	1,394,516	1,000,000
Japan	33,623,319	50,661,878
Algiers	2,867,626	5,790,000
Total 16 countries.	275,537,110	$1,045,697,480

Only 9 countries use gold to the exclusion of silver, and 8 of these have in circulation $126,654,747 silver, with a limited legal tender quality. There are 16 countries using both gold and silver as legal tender and one silver exclusively. The population of the 9 gold using countries is 55,527,216, while that of the 17 silver using countries is 466,200,733, more than eight times as many. The gold used by the gold countries amounts to $735,839,519, while the silver used in the silver and the gold and silver using countries, having full legal tender quality, amounts to $2,-060,697,480, more than 2 4-5 times as much as gold. The entire amount of gold in circulation in all countries is $2,819,303,004, and the full legal tender silver is $2,060,697,480 or over 70 per cent. of the gold circulation. The amount of silver, full and limited legal tender, in circulation, is $2,482,950,021, or within 15 per cent. of as much as gold.

The countries using gold exclusively, or giving to silver a limited legal tender power only, are as follows :

	Population.	Am't of Gold.
Great Britain...... ..	31,628,338	$596,019,721
Canada..........	4,075,000	6,291,285
Australia.........	2,603,000	60,821,147
Greece...........	1,679,775	4,500,000
Sweden...........	4,429,713	7,158,000
Norway...........	1,806,900	3,233,366
Denmark..........	1,912,142	9,316,000
Portugal.......... ..	4,441,037	48,000,000
Columbia.........	2,951,311	500,000
Total 9 countries.	55,527,216	$735,839,519

COINAGE OF UNITED STATES MINTS.

The total coinage executed in the United States from the organization of the mint (1793) to the close of the fiscal year ended June 30, 1880, was as follows:

GOLD.

Double Eagles..................	$919,754,480
Eagles.......................	76,730,470
Half Eagles..................	87,334,485
Three Dollars...............	1,556,154
Quarter Eagles..............	28,374,525
Dollars.....................	19,353,208
Total gold...............	$1,133,103,322

SILVER.

Trade Dollars................	$35,959,360	00
Dollars.....................	71,780,588	00
Half Dollars................	122,748,295	50
Quarter Dollars.............	38,481,099	00
Twenty Cents................	271,000	00
Dimes.......................	16,904,297	30
Half Dimes..................	4,906,946	90
Three Cents.................	1,281,850	20
Total silver...............	$292,333,436	90

MINOR.

Five Cents..................	$5,775,592	50
Three Cents.................	857,104	50
Two Cents...................	912,020	00
One Cent....................	5,698,523	94
Half Cents..................	39,926	11
Total minor...............	$13,283,167	05

SUMMARY.

Gold.......................	$1,133,103,322	00
Silver.....................	292,333,436	90
Minor......................	13,283,167	05
Total coinage...........	$1,438,719,925	95

The coinage executed at the mints of the United States during the year 1880 was as follows:

Double eagles....................	$17,749,120	00
Eagles	21,690,160	00
Half eagles......................	22,831,765	00
Three dollars....................	3,108	00
Quarter eagles..................	7,490	00
Dollars........................	1,636	00
Total gold..................	$62,283,279	00
Dollars........................	$27,397,355	00
Half dollars....................	4,877	50
Quarter dollars.................	3,738	75
Dimes	3,735	50
Total silver.................	$27,409,706	75
Five cents......................	997	75
Three cents.....................	748	65
Cents	389,649	55
Total subsidiary.............	$391,395	95
Grand total.................	$90,084,381	70

The coinage of gold in the United States reached its maximum in 1851, when $62,613,492.50 were coined. The average coinage of gold during the past ten years was $39,000 per annum; and the aggregate amount since 1793 was $1,133,103,322. During the years 1816 and 1817 no gold coins were struck off. The coinage of silver reached its maximum in 1877, when $28,549,935 was coined. The aggregate since 1793 is $292,333,436.90, or a little more than 25 per cent. of the gold coinage. In no year has there been a total cessation of the coinage of silver, although at several times the amount has been reduced to below $1,000,000 in a year, and in 1864 to only $548,214.10. The silver coinage during the past six years amounted to $141,207,951, or nearly one-half of the entire amount turned out since the mints were organized.

The movement of silver in the United States from January 1, 1878, to September 30, 1880, embracing the period from the time the Bland silver bill was passed, down to the latest date when complete returns can be had, is shown in the following figures : The imports of American silver coin, including trade dollars, amounted to $12,040,243, and the exports to $3,667,972, leaving as net imports $8,372,271. The imports of bullion (foreign and domestic) and foreign coin amounted to $29,972,118, and the exports to $43,762,095, leaving as net exports $13,729,977. The coinage of standard silver dollars during the same period amounted to $70,555,650.

The following table shows the monthly excess of imports over exports of coin and bullion into the United States during the year 1880 compared with 1879 :

	1879.	1880.
January..........	*$669,834	$165,565
February........	*300,145	279,762
March..........	*1,876,090	106,290
April...........	*2,452,655	725,643
May...........	*882,592	*583,294
June...........	*1,462,289	177,860
July...........	59,273	324,451
August..........	5,935,477	9,238,339
September.......	27,130,587	19,104,049
October....	18,728,342	14,552,138
November.... ...	17,288,564	9,374,865
December....	5,877,322	15,764,154
Total............$67,375,960		$69,229,822

* Excess of exports.

The following is an estimate of the gold and silver coin and bullion in the country Oct. 1, 1880, and its distribution :

Gold coin in the country June 30. '79 $286,490.698 00
Coinage of the mints (15 months).. 66,723.499 00
Net import of U. S. gold coin (14 mos.) 16,666,806 00

Total gold.................$369,881.003 00
Silver coin in the country June 30, '79 $112,050,985 00
Coinage of the mints (15 months).. 34,776.437 50
Net import U. S. silver coin (14 m'ths) 2,971,913 00

Total silver.................149,799.335 50

DISTRIBUTION.

	Coin in the Treasury.	Coin in Circulation and Banks.	Total.
Gold.	67,204,293 65	302,676,709 35	369,881,003 00
Silver.	72,454,600 00	77,344,735 50	149,799,335 50
To'l	139,658,93 658	380,021.444 85	519,680,338 50

Uncoined gold bullion in the Treasury 68.040.540 00
"   silver "   "   "   5.557.759 74

Total gold and silver coin and bullion
  available for coinage.........$593.278.638 24

The following is a comparative statement of the production of gold and silver in the United States for the fiscal years ending June 30th, 1877, 1878 and 1879.

GOLD.

Locality.	1877.	1878.	1879.
California....	.$15,000,000	$15,260,679	$17,600,000
Nevada......	18,000,000	19,546,513	9,000,000
Montana......	3,200,000	2,260,511	2,500,000
Idaho........	1,500,000	1,150,000	1,200,000
Utah........	350,000	392,00	575,000
Colorado.....	3,000,000	3,366,440	3,225,000
Arizona......	300,000	500,000	800,000
New Mexico..	175,000	175,000	125,000
Oregon.......	1,000,000	1,000,000	1,150,000
Washington...	300,000	300,000	75,000
Dakota.......	2,000,000	2,000,000	2,420,000
Virginia......	50,000	....	....
North Carolina	100,000	150,000	90,000
Georgia......	100,000	100,000	90,000
Other sources.	25,000	25,000	50,000
	$45,100,000	47,266,107	38,900,000

SILVER.

California.....	.$1,000,000	$2,273,380	$2,400,000
Nevada	26,000,000	28,130,350	12,560,000
Montana.....	750,000	1,669,635	2,225,000
Idado........	250,000	200,000	650,000
Utah...... ...	5,075,000	5,208,000	6,250,000
Colorado.....	4,500,000	5,304,940	11,700,000
Arizona......	500,000	3,000,000	3,350,000
New Mexico..	500,000	500,000	600,000
Oregon.......	100,000	100,000	20,000
Washington...	50,000	26,000	20,000
Dakota.......	....	....	60,000
Lake Superior.	200,000	100,000	780,000
Other sources.	25,000	25,000	47,000
	38,950,000	46,726,314	40,812,000

DIRECTORY

OF

TRANSFER OFFICES, BANKS, ETC.

NAME.	TRANSFER OFFICE.
Alabama Central	52 William street.
Albany and Susquehanna	Bank of Commerce.
Atchison, Colorado and Pacific	111 William street.
Atchison, Topeka and Santa Fe	Bank of Commerce.
Atlantic and Charlotte Air Line	Coal and Iron Exchange.
Boston and New York Air Line	12 Wall street.
Boston, Hartford and Erie	3 Pine street.
Brunswick and Albany	53 Exchange place.
Buffalo, New York and Erie	9 Nassau street.
Burlington, Cedar Rapids and Northern	56 Broadway.
Cairo and Vincennes	3 Broad street.
Carolina Central	Farmers Loan and Trust Co.
Cayuga and Susquehanna	26 Exchange place.
Cedar Falls and Minnesota	41 Cedar street.
Central Pacific	9 Nassau street.
Central of Georgia	National City Bank.
Central of Minnesota	92 Broadway.
Central of New Jersey	119 Liberty street.
Chatfield	52 Wall street.
Cherry Valley, Sharon and Albany	Coal and Iron Exchange.
Chesapeake and Ohio	9 Nassau street.
Chester	Farmers Loan and Trust Co.
Chicago and Alton	35 William street.
Chicago, Burlington and Quincy	National Bank of Commerce.
Chicago and Canada Southern	Grand Central Depot.
Chicago and Eastern Illinois	Union Trust Company.
Chicago, Milwaukee and St. Paul	68 William street.
Chicago and Northwestern	52 Wall street.
Chicago and Paducah	80 Broadway.
Chicago, Rock Island and Pacific	13 William street.
Chicago, St. Louis and New Orleans	31 Nassau street.
Chicago, St. Paul, Minneapolis and Omaha	5 Exchange court.
Cincinnati, Ind. St. Louis and Chicago	American Exchange Bank.
Cincinnati, Sandusky and Cleveland	Union Trust Company.
Cincinnati, Cumberland Gap and Charleston	2 Exchange court.
Cleveland and Pittsburg	26 Exchange place.
Cleveland, Columbus, Cincinnati and Indianapolis	Union Trust Company.
Columbus, Chicago and Indiana Central	Union Trust Company.
Cumberland and Pennsylvania	Union Trust Co.
Danbury and Norwalk	84 Broadway.
Delaware and Hudson Canal	Bank of Commerce.
Delaware, Lackawanna and Western	26 Exchange place.
Denison and Southeastern	98 Broadway.
Denver and Rio Grande	Coal and Iron Exchange.
Des Moines and Fort Dodge	61 Wall street.
Easton and Amboy	Coal and Iron Exchange.
Elizabeth, Lexington and Big Sandy	9 Nassau street.

Erie and Pittsburg...................................Union Trust Company.
Elizabeth City and Norfolk.........................United Bank Building.
Freehold and New York............................61 Wall street.
Geneva and Lyons..................................Grand Central Depot.
Georgia Southern...................................52 Broadway.
Grand Rapids and Indiana..........................27 Pine street.
Greene..26 Exchange place,
Hannibal and St. Joseph............................80 Broadway.
Harlem Extension, South............................57 Liberty street.
Harlem River and Portchester......................Grand Central Depot.
Hastings and Dakota................................80 Broadway.
High Bridge.........................·..............119 Liberty street.
Houston and Texas Central.........................80 Wall street.
Illinois Central.....................................Union Trust Company.
Indiana, Bloomington and Western.................115 Broadway.
Indianapolis, Decatur and Springfield..............120 Broadway.
International and Great Northern...................49 Cedar street.
Iowa Midland.......................................52 Wall street.
Ithica, Auburn and Western........................20 Nassau street.
Junction and Breakwater...........................197 Greenwich street.
Junction (Buffalo)..................................Grand Central Depot.
Keokuk and Des Moines............................13 William street.
Lackawanna and Susquehanna......................Coal and Iron Exchange.
Lake Champlain and Moriah....·...................56 Broadway.
Lake Erie and Western.............................Metropolitan National Bank.
Lake Shore and Michigan Southern.................Grand Central Depot.
Long Branch and Sea Girt..........................119 Liberty street.
Long Wood Valley..................................119 Liberty street.
Louisiana and Missouri River.......................54 William street.
Louisville and Nashville............................52 Wall street.
Louisville, New Albany and Chicago................26 Exchange place.
Lykens Valley.......................................13 William street.
Manhattan Elevated................................71 Broadway.
Marietta and Cincinnati.............................26 Exchange place.
Memphis and Charleston............................2 Exchange court.
Metropolitan Elevated..............................Central Trust Co.
Michigan Central...................................Grand Central Depot.
Michigan, Midland and Canada....................Grand Central Depot.
Minnesota Valley...................................52 Wall street.
Missouri, Kansas and Texas........................80 Broadway.
Missouri Pacific....................................80 Broadway.
Missouri and Western..............................3 Broad street.
Mobile and Montgomery............................52 Wall street.
Mobile and Ohio....................................9 Nassau street.
Morris and Essex...................................26 Exchange place.
Nashville, Chattanooga and St. Louis..............Continental National Bank.
Newark and Bloomfield............................26 Exchange place.
Newark and Hudson...............................Coal and Iron Exchange.
Newburg and New York............................Coal and Iron Exchange.
New Egypt and Farmingdale.......................119 Liberty street.
New Jersey Southern...............................119 Liberty street.
New York, Bay Ridge and Jamaica.................61 Broadway.
New York and Canada.............................Coal and Iron Exchange.
New York Central and Hudson River.............Grand Central Depot.
New York City and Northern.......................3 Broad street.
New York Elevated.................................7 Broadway.
New York and Greenwood Lake....................197 Reade street.
New York and Harlem..............................Grand Central Depot.
New York, Housatonic and Northern..............74 Wall street.
New York, Lake Erie and Western................Coal and Iron Exchange.

New York and Long Branch.........................119 Liberty street.
New York and Mahopac............................Grand Central Depot.
New York and Manhattan Beach....................115 Broadway.
New York, New Haven and Hartford................Grand Central Depot.
New York, Ontario and Western...................Third National Bank.
New York, Providence and Boston.................39 William street.
Northern Pacific................................23 Fifth avenue.
Nyack and Northern..............................197 Reade street.
Ohio Central...................................Metropolitan National Bank.
Ohio and Mississippi...........................54 William street.
Oregon Railway and Navigation..................20 Nassau street.
Oswego and Syracuse............................20 Nassau street.
Panama...37 Wall street.
Passaic and Delaware...........................26 Exchange place.
Paterson and Hudson River......................Church and Cortlandt sts.
Pennsylvania...................................21 Cortlandt street.
Philadelphia and Reading.......................26 Exchange place.
Pittsburg, Fort Wayne and Chicago..............24 Nassau street.
Port Royal and Augusta.........................252 Broadway.
Rensselaer and Saratoga........................Bank of Commerce.
Richmond and Alleghany.........................3 Broad street.
Rome, Watertown and Ogdensburg.................26 Exchange place.
St. Joseph and St. Louis.......................80 Broadway.
St. Louis, Alton and Terre Haute...............50 Wall street.
St. Louis Bridge...............................3 Broadway.
St. Louis, Iron Mountain and Southern..........Farmers' Loan &"Trust Co.
St. Louis and San Francisco....................3 Broad street.
St. Paul, Minneapolis and Manitoba.............63 William street.
Savannah, Florida and Western..................12 W. 23d street.
Schenectady and Duanesburg.....................Coal and Iron Exchange.
Southern Minnesota.............................92 Broadway.
Southfield Branch..............................42 Pine street.
Spuyten Duyvil and Port Morris.................Grand Central Depot.
Staten Island..................................Foot of Whitehall street.
Sterling Mountain..............................42 Pine street.
Suspension Bridge and Erie Junction............Church and Cortlandt sts.
Sussex...26 Exchange place.
Syracuse Junction..............................Grand Central Depot.
Texas and New Orleans..........................54 Exchange place.
Texas and Pacific..............................26 Exchange place.
Texas Western..................................141 Broadway.
Tunnel of St. Louis............................3 Broad street.
Union Pacific..................................Union Trust Company.
Utica, Clinton and Susquehanna.................26 Exchange place.
Valley, New York...............................26 Exchange place.
Vineland.......................................119 Liberty street.
Wabash, St. Louis and Pacific..................80 Broadway.
Warren...26 Exchange place.
Wasatch and Jordan Valley......................115 Broadway.
Waverly and State Line.........................Coal and Iron Exchange.
West Troy and Green Island.....................Coal and Iron Exchange.
Winona, Mankota and New Ulm....................52 Wall street.
Winona and St. Peter...........................52 Wall street.

MINING COMPANIES.

NAME.	TRANSFER OFFICE.	NAME.	TRANSFER OFF'E.
Alice	47 Broadway.	Great Eastern	31 Broad st.
Alta Montana	18 Wall st.	Green Mountain	18 Wall st.
American Cons	31 Broad st.	Harshaw	62 Pearl st.
American Flag	59 William st.	Hibernia Cons	115 Broadway.
Amie	115 Broadway.	Homestake	18 Wall st.
Argenta	115 Broadway.	Horn Silver	44 Wall st.
Atlantic Copper	74 Wall st.	Hortense	57 Broadway.
Auburn&RockCreek	115 Broadway.	Hukill	115 Broadway.
Bald Mountain	21 Nassau st.	Iron Silver	8 Wall st.
Barbee & Walker	59 Drexel Building.	Kings Mountain	52 Broadway.
Barcelona	115 Broadway.	Lacrosse	59 William st.
Bassick	44 Wall st.	La Plata	58 Broadway.
Battle Creek	115 Broadway.	Leadville Cons	115 Broadway.
Bechtel	115 Broadway.	Legal Tender	63 Broadway.
Big Pittsburg	137 Broadway.	Little Chief	137 Broadway.
Black Jack	18 Wall st.	Little Pittsburg	115 Broadway.
Bodie	12 Pine st.	Lowland Chief	115 Broadway.
Bonanza Chief	16 Wall st.	Lucerne	60 Broadway.
Boston Cons	61 Broadway.	Malachite	115 Broadway.
Boulder Cons	62 Broadway.	Mariposa	9 Nassau st.
Breece	115 Broadway.	Mayflower	161 Broadway.
Buckeye	52 Broadway.	Mineral Creek	115 Broadway.
Bull Domingo	115 Broadway.	Miner Boy	63 Broadway.
Bulwer	52 Broadway.	Moose	57 Broadway.
Bye-and-Bye	115 Broadway.	Moose Silver	62 Broadway.
Calaveras	25 Broad st.	Morning Star	81 Cedar st.
Carbonate Hill	4 Pine st.	O. K. & Winnebago.	Drexel Building.
Caribou Cons	33 Broad st.	Ontario	18 Wall st.
Central Arizona	Union Trust Co.	Original Keystone	1 Wall st.
Cherokee	18 Wall st.	Pelican & Dives	197 Broadway.
Cheyenne	54 Broadway.	Plumas	54 Broad st.
Chrysolite	18 Wall st.	Quicksilver	19 Nassau st.
Climax	62 Broadway.	Rappahannock	60 Broadway.
Colorado Central	29 Broad st.	Red Elephant	31 Broad st.
Columbia Cons	33 Wall st.	Rico	115 Broadway.
ConsolidatedArizona	145 Broadway.	Rising Sun	18 Wall st.
Copper Knob	52 Broadway.	Robinson Cons	206 Broadway.
Crowell	52 Broadway.	Sacramento	62 Broadway.
Dahlonega	115 Broadway.	Silver Cliff	30 Broad st.
Deadwood	18 Wall st.	Silver Islet	52 Broadway.
Dunderberg	62 Broadway.	Silver King, Col	60 Broadway.
Dunkin	60 Broad st.	Silver Nugget	52 Broadway.
Durango	115 Broadway.	South Bulwer	35 Broadway.
Empire	58 Broadway.	South Hite	35 Broadway,
Eureka Cons	58 Broadway.	South Noonday	35 Broadway.
Evening Star	33 Wall st.	Spring Valley	61 Broadway.
Excelsior	18 Wall st.	Standard Cons	67 New st.
Father De Smet	12 Pine st.	Starr-Grove	2 Nassau st.
Findley	70 Broadway.	Stormont	2 Nassau st.
Freeland	115 Broadway.	Trio	10 Wall st.
Glass Pendery	115 Broadway.	Unadilla	52 Broadway.
Gold Placer	57 Broadway.	Union Cons	35 Broadway.
Gold Stripe	18 Wall st.	Vandewater	115 Broadway.
Grand View	115 Broadway.	Willshire	60 Wall st.
Granville	23 Dey st.		

BANKS—NATIONAL.

American Exchange	128 Broadway.	Leather Manufacturers	29 Wall st.
Bank of Commerce	31 Nassau st.	Marine	78 Wall st.
Bank of New York	48 Wall st.	Market	286 Pearl st.
Bank of the Republic	2 Wall st.	Mechanics	33 Wall st.
Bank of the State of N.Y.	31 William st.	Mechanics Banking Asso	38 Wall st.
Bowery	62 Bowery.	Mechanics and Traders	153 Bowery.
Broadway	237 Broadway.	Mercantile	191 Broadway.
Butchers and Drovers	124 Bowery.	Merchants	42 Wall st.
Central	322 Broadway.	Merchants Exchange	257 Broadway.
Chase	104 Broadway.	Metropolitan	108 Broadway.
Chatham	196 Broadway.	New York County	14 st. & 8 ave.
Chemical	270 Broadway.	New York Exchange	136 Chambers.
Citizens	401 Broadway.	Ninth	409 Broadway.
City	52 Wall st.	Park	216 Broadway.
Continental	7 Nassau st.	Phenix	45 Wall st.
East River	682 Broadway.	St. Nicholas	Wall & New st.
Fifth	3d ave. c. 23d.	Second	190 Fifth ave.
First	94 Broadway.	Seventh Ward	234 Pearl st.
Fourth	16 Nassau st.	Shoe and Leather	271 Broadway.
Fulton	39 Fulton st.	Sixth	1330 Broadway
Gallatin	36 Wall st.	Third	20 Nassau st.
Hanover	11 Nassau st.	Tradesmens	291 Broadway.
Importers and Traders	247 Broadway.	Union	34 Wall st.
Irving	287 Greenwich.	United States	35 Nassau st.

BANKS—STATE.

Bank of America	46 Wall st.	Manhattan Company	40 Wall st.
Bank of North America	44 Wall st.	Mount Morris	133 E. 125th st
Bank of the Metropolis	17 Union sq.	Murray Hill	760 Third ave.
Corn Exchange	13 William st.	Nassau	137 Nassau st.
Eleventh Ward	147 Ave. D.	North River	187 Greenwich
Fifth Avenue	44 st. & 5th a.	Oriental	122 Bowery.
German American	50 Wall st.	Pacific	470 Broadway.
German Exchange	245 Bowery.	Peoples	395 Canal st.
Germania	330 Bowery.	Produce	59 Barclay st.
Greenwich	402 Hudson st.	West Side	491 8th ave.
Island City	79 W. 23d st.		

New York Clearing House Association.......14 Pine street, cor. Nassau street.

BANKS—SAVINGS.

Bank for Savings	67 Bleecker st.	Harlem	2281 3d ave.
Bowery	128 Bowery.	Institution for the Savings	
Broadway Savings Inst'n.	4 Park place.	of Merchants' Clerks.	20 Union sq.
Citizens	58 Bowery.	Irving	96 Warren st.
Dry Dock	343 Bowery.	Manhattan Savings Ins'n	644 Broadway.
East River	3 Chambers st.	Metropolitan	1 Third ave.
East Side for Sailors	187 Cherry st.	Morrisania	3d a. c. Court'd
Eleventh Ward	908 Third ave.	New York	81 8th ave.
Emigrant Industrial	51 Chambers.	North River	476 8th ave.
Exsicelor	374 Sixth ave.	St. Johns	Fordham.
Franklin	658 8th ave.	Seamen's	74 Wall st.
German	157 4th ave.	Union Dime	54 W. 32d st.
Greenwich	73 Sixth ave.	West Side	154 Sixth ave.

TRUST COMPANIES.

Ameri'n Dock and Trust.110 Pearl st.
Central...................15 Nassau st.
Equitable................27 Pine st.
Farmers Loan and Trust.26 Exchange p.
Mercantile......,........120 Broadway.
Mining Trust.............115 Broadway.

N.Y. Life Ins'ce & Trust.52 Wall st.
Real Estate.... ....115 Broadway.
Union...................73 Broadway.
United States............49 Wall st.
United States Mortgage..50 Wall st.

SAFE DEPOSIT COMPANIES.

Bank of N. Y. Safe De-
  posit Vaults..:..........48 Wall st.
Central..................71 & 73 W. 23
Mercantile...............120 Broadway.

Safe Deposit Co. of N. Y.140 Broadway.'
Safe Deposit Vault of the
  National Park Bank....214 Broadway.
Stuyvesant...............3d ave. c. 7 st.

EXCHANGES.

New York Stock.....................................12 Broad street.
New York Mining Stock............................60 Broadway.
American Mining Stock... ....63 Broadway.
New York Produce...............................Whitehall and Pearl streets.
New York Cotton.................................Hanover Square.
New York Petroleum.............................23 William street.
Maritime...66 Beaver street.

MISCELLANEOUS COMPANIES.

Adams Express.....................................57 Broadway.
American Express..................................61 Broadway.
American District Telegraph......................123 So. 5th Ave.
American Union Telegraph.......................80 Broadway.
Atlantic and Pacific Telegraph...................145 Broadway.
Boston Water Power...............................Astor House.
Boston Land........ .... .45 Broad St.
Canton Land.......................................111 Broadway.
Colorado Coal and Iron...........................Coal and Iron Exchange.
Delaware and Hudson Canal......................Bank of Commerce.
Long Dock...187 Water St.
Maryland Coal.....................................111 Broadway.
Montauk Coal and Gas...........................111 Broadway.
Pacific Mail Steamship...........................Union Trust Co.
Pullman Palace Car...............................3 Broad St.
Western Union Telegraph........................Union Trust Co.